GOLDEN Treasury of KNOWLEDGE

Chief Editor
Biman Basu

PENTAGON PRESS

GOLDEN Treasury of Knowledge

ISBN 81-8274-962-X

First Published in India in 2006

Published by
PENTAGON PRESS
A-38, Hauz Khas, Delhi-16
Phones : 011-51656996, 8, 51517091, Tele fax : 011-51656997
Email : pentagonpress@touchtelindia.net
Website : www.pentagon-press.com

Designed by
GLOW WORMS

Printed and bound by Brijbasi Art Press Ltd.

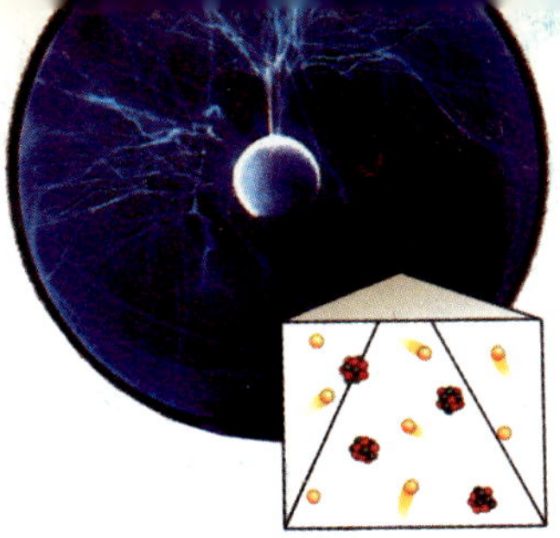

CONTENTS

UNIT - 1

UNIT - 2

UNIT - 3

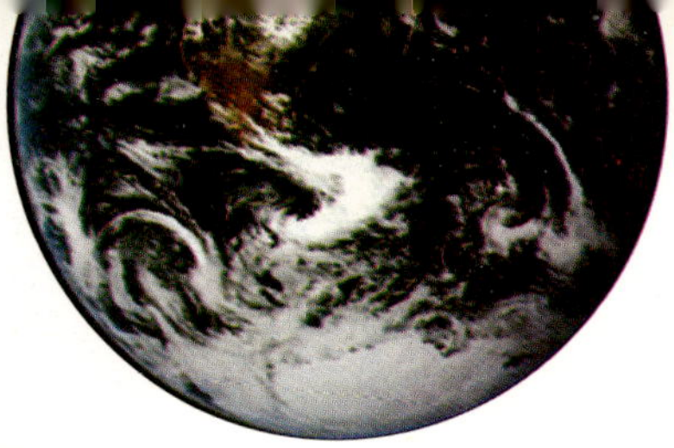

UNIT - 4

UNIT-5

GOLDEN Treasury of Knowledge

- Matter
- Atoms
- Elements
- Radioactivity
- Forces and Energy
- Light
- Sound
- Magnetism and Electricity
- Air and Atmosphere
- Water
- Ecology
- Cycles in Nature
- Producers
- Consumers
- Decomposers
- Food Chain and Food Web
- Our Body
- Sense Organs
- Respiration and Digestion
- Nervous and Muscular System
- Skeleton and Bones
- Excretion and Reproduction
- Heart
- Energy from Food

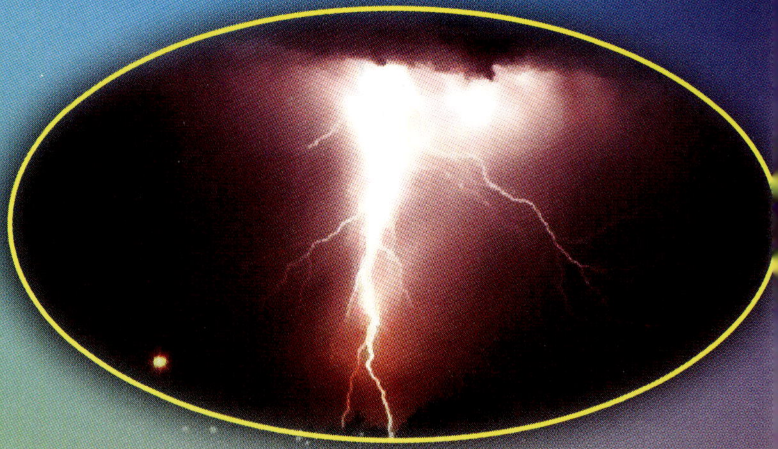

Unit – 1

Science World

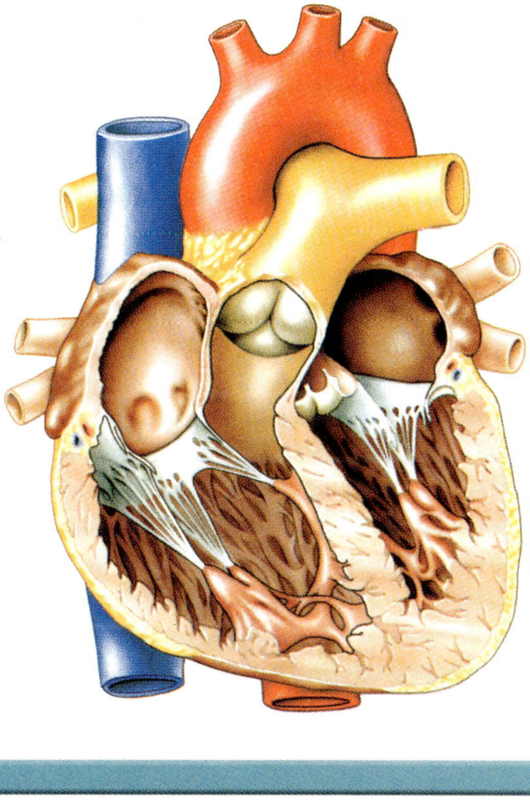

Matter

Matter is all the material in the Universe. The matter around us on Earth is made up of atoms in the form of solids, liquids and gases. There are three normal states of matter, that are solid, liquid and gas. Usually substances can exist in all three states, depending on the temperature.

Solids

Substances at low temperatures are solids. Solids have fixed shape and volume. The particles in solids are packed tightly. The particles of this state can vibrate when dropped, though powerful forces hold them tightly in place.
To exchange the shape of solids is nearly impossible.

Different solid articles.

Different liquids

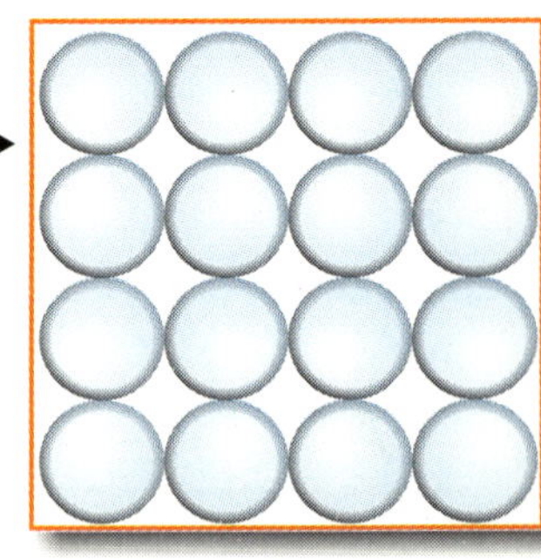

Particles in solids are tightly packed together. They attract one another so strongly that they cannot move about, they only vibrate.

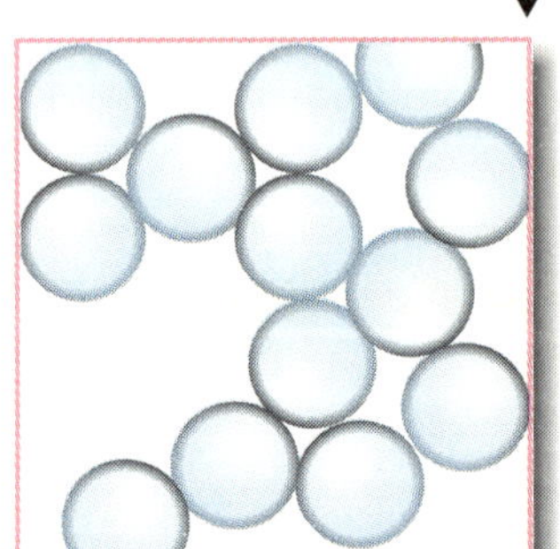

Particles in liquids are grouped in clusters.

Liquids

If a solid is heated it finally melts to form a liquid. Liquids do not have a definite shape. They take shape of the container they are in. The particles of liquids are more loosely packed than solids. A liquid takes the shape of its container, thus it will change its shape every time you pour it in different container.

Gases

At even higher temperatures, a liquid boils to form a gas or vapour. There is no definite shape and volume of a gas, it will expand to fill its container. The particles of gas are very loosely packed. The particles move very freely as the bonds between the particles are very weak.

Liquid boils to form a gas.

A boy filling air in the balloon.

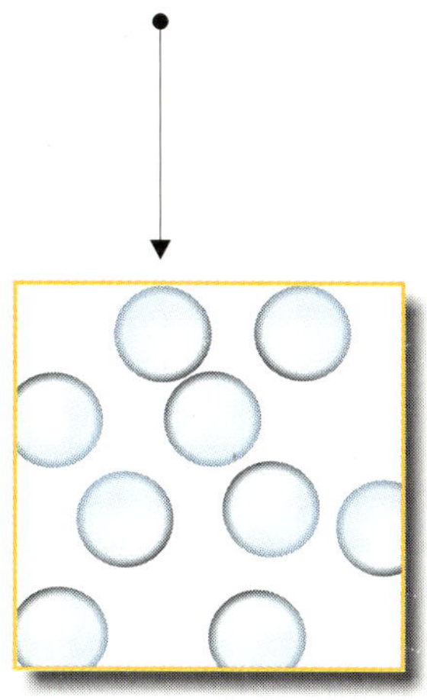

Particles in gases are loosely packed.

AMAZING FACT !

Plasma is only found at very high temperatures such as inside the sun and other stars.

The fourth state of matter Plasma

You may be surprised to learn about the fourth state of matter. It is true that there exists another state of matter besides the three. It is known as plasma. Plasma develops when electrons are torn from their atoms by electricity or heat.

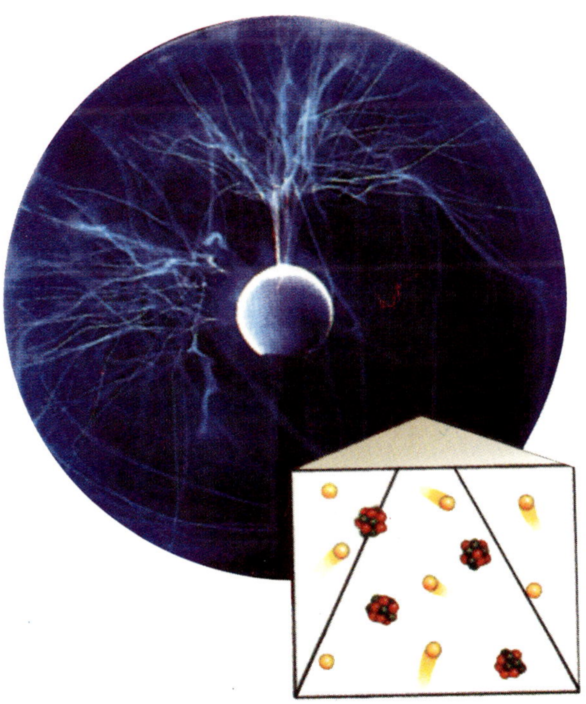

Plasma is the fourth state of matter.

Atoms

An atom is a minute unit of matter. Atoms are so small that around a million of them would fit onto a dot. Everything around us is made up of atoms. Atoms comprise even tinier particles known as protons, neutrons and electrons.

Atomic Number

The atomic number of chemical element gives us the number of positive charges or protons, or negative charges or electrons there are in the atom. The number is the same for both, so the atom has no charge. For example, carbon has six protons and six electrons, therefore its atomic number is six. The atoms of the 90 naturally-occurring elements can be placed in order by arranging them according to their atomic numbers.

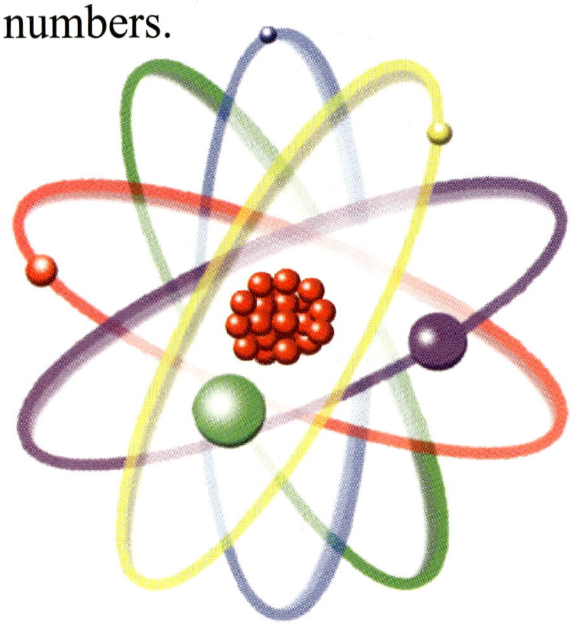

Atoms and sub atomic particles are not solid - they are clouds of energy.

AMAZING FACT !

If an atom were the size of our little finger nail then your hand would be large enough to hold the Earth.

Element	Atomic Number
Nitrogen	7
Oxygen	8
Aluminium	13
Sulphur	16
Calcium	20

Milestones in the study of the atom

400s BC	*Democritus* gave the name atom to the basic particle.
1750	*Boscovich* believed atoms are made up of even smaller parts.
1803	*Dalton* proposed that each element has its own particular type of atom.
1911	*Rutherford* proposed that most of the mass of an atom is concentrated in a small nucleus consisting of protons, which is surrounded by electrons travelling at great speed.
1932	*Chadwick* discovered that the nucleus contains neutrons.
1938	Nuclear fission is discovered.
1971	Quarks identified. Shown to be smaller than protons and neutrons.
1988	Positron (anti-electron) microscope in use.

The man who gave Atomic Theory

John Dalton was an English chemist. He is best known for his atomic theory to explain the structure of matter. It became one of the foundations of modern chemistry. He was the first to calculate the weights of the atoms of several elements.

Electrons constantly change their positions as they whizz round a nucleus of protons and neutrons, making billions of trips in one millionth of a second.

John Dalton

Elements

A chemical element is a substance in which all the atoms are of the same kind. Elements cannot be broken down into simpler substances, but in certain nuclear reactions one element can be changed into another.

Elements known

There are as of 2005, 116 known elements, only 90 of which naturally, most of them are found as compounds, the rest 26 are derived artificially in controlled nuclear reactions.

Periodic Table

The Periodic Table comprises all the known elements in order of increasing atomic number. Elements of atoms with similar structures have similar properties and so are positioned close.

1	2	3	4	5	6	7	8
1 Hydrogen H							
3 Lithium Li	4 Beryllium Be						
11 Sodium Na	12 Magnesium Mg						
19 Potassium K	20 Calcium Ca	21 Scandium Sc	22 Titanium Ti	23 Vanadium V	24 Chromium Cr	25 Manganese Mn	26 Iron Fe
37 Rubidium Rb	38 Strontium Sr	39 Yttrium Y	40 Zirconium Zr	41 Niobium Nb	42 Molybdenum Mo	43 Technetium Tc	44 Ruthen Ru
55 Caesium Cs	56 Barium Ba	57-71 Lanthanide series	72 Hafnium Hf	73 Tantalum Ta	74 Tungsten W	75 Rhenium Re	76 Osmi Os
87 Francium Fr	88 Radium Ra	89-103 Actinide series	104 Rutherfordium Rf	105 Dubrium Db	106 Seaborgium Sg	107 Bohrium Bh	108 Hassi Hs

57 Lanthanum La	58 Cerium Ce	59 Praseodymium Pr	60 Neodymium Nd	61 Prometheum Pm	62 Samarium Sm	63 Europium eu	64 Gadolir Gd
89 Actinium Ac	90 Thorium Th	91 Protactinium Pa	92 Uranium U	93 Neptunium Np	94 Plutonium Pu	95 Americium Am	96 Curiu Cm

The creator of First Periodic Table

Mendeleyev was a Russian chemist who drew up the first periodic table. He did this by charting the known chemical elements in order of increasing atomic weight.

Dmitri Mendeleyev

Out of all the elements known, 90 occur naturally on Earth. Gold, silver, mercury and copper are a few of them.

AMAZING FACT !

Ancient Greek philosophers believed there were just four elements: earth, fire, air and water.

Gold

Silver

Copper

9	10	11	12	13	14	15	16	17	18
									2 Helium He
				5 Boron B	6 Carbon C	7 Nitrogen N	8 Oxygen O	9 Fluorine F	10 Neon Ne
				13 Aluminium Al	14 Silicon Si	15 Phosphorus P	16 Sulphur S	17 Chlorine Cl	18 Argon Ar
27 Cobalt Co	28 Nickel Ni	29 Copper Cu	30 Zinc Zn	31 Gallium Ga	32 Germanium Ge	33 Arsenic As	34 Selenium Se	35 Bromine Br	36 Krypton Kr
45 Rhodium Rh	46 Palladium Pd	47 Silver Ag	48 Cadmium Cd	49 Indium In	50 Tin Sn	51 Antimony Sb	52 Tellurium Te	53 Iodine I	54 Xenon Xe
77 Iridium Ir	78 Platinum Pt	79 Gold Au	80 Mercury Hg	81 Thallium Tl	82 Lead Pb	83 Bismuth Bi	84 Polonium Po	85 Astatine At	86 Radon Rn
109 eitnerium Mt	110 Damstadtium Ds	111 Roentgenium Rg	112 Ununbium Uub	113 Ununtrium Uut	114 Ununquadium Uuq	115 Ununpentium Uup	116 Ununhesium Uuh		

This chart arranges elements into "groups" (columns) and "periods" (rows).

65 Terbium Tb	66 Dysprosium Dy	67 Holmium Ho	68 Erbium Er	69 Thulium Tm	70 Ytterbium Yb	71 Lutetium Lu
97 erkelium Bk	98 Californium Cf	99 Einsteinium Es	100 Fermium Fm	101 Mendelevium Md	102 Nobelium No	103 Lawrencium Lr

Periodic Table

Radioactivity 

Radioactivity describes the tiny subatomic particles and high-energy rays that are given out by the nuclei of certain atoms. There are at least three types of radioactive emissions called alpha, beta and gamma radiation.

Alpha radiation

Alpha radiation consists of two protons and two neutrons bound together, identical to the nucleus of a helium atom.

Beta radiation

Beta radiation consists of electrons and is produced when a neutron inside the nucleus turns into a proton. Both alpha and beta radioactivity change the atomic number of the atom left behind.

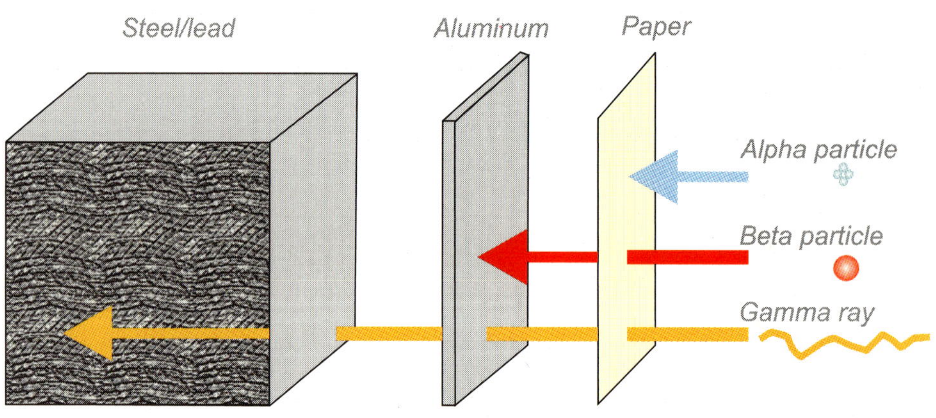

Radiation chart

Gamma radiation

Gamma radiation consists of electromagnetic radiation of very high frequency. Gamma radiation does not change the type of nucleus that is left behind and penetrates further than alpha and beta particles.

SI units

Radioactivity is measured in units called becquerels, named after the French scientist *Henri Becquerel* who discovered radioactivity. The SI unit for radiation dosage or exposure is the sievert, named after the Swedish physicist *Rolf Sievert*.

Radioactive Half-Lives

Radioactivity is a random process, it is not possible to say when a particular atom will give out a particle or ray. It is possible, however, given a large number of atoms to say how long it will be before half of them have decayed, this time is called the Half-Life.

AMAZING FACT !

A brief pulse of electric current flows when a radioactive particle enters a Geiger counter. The radioactivity of a sample is calculated by the number of these pulses.

Geiger counter

Man behind the discovery

Becquerel was a French physicist who in 1896 discovered radioactivity. He found that radiation given off by uranium salts fogged photographic plates. He went on to investigate the radiation, and three years later proved that some of it consisted of charged particles. For this work he shared the 1903 Nobel Prize in Physics with Pierre and Marie Curie, the discoverers of radium.

Henri Becquerel

Forces and Energy

A force is a push or a pull that acts on an object. There are forces all around us. Forces require energy. Energy is the ability to do work. When you perform a particular task, energy is used or converted from one form to another.

Force

A force is something that pushes or pulls an object in a particular direction. Issac Newton realized that if one object produces a force on another, the first object experiences an equal and opposite reaction force. He also realized that forces cause objects to accelerate.

Force is a push or a pull that acts on a body.

Einstein's theory of Relativity

Albert Einstein, the German American physicist, stated that gravity is a property of space rather than a force of attraction between bodies of matter.

Albert Einstein

Energy

Energy is required when a force is to be moved through some distance. Such a process involves doing work; energy is the ability to do work and it is measured in joules. Energy is conserved, the total amount of energy never changes, but it is converted from one form to another.

Energy is required to do work.

AMAZING FACT !

The Sun gives off light energy from 150 million km away. This is known as Solar Energy. We use this energy to perform various tasks.

Types of energy

If an object is moving, this gives it a form of energy known as kinetic energy. Heat is also a form of energy; kinetic energy is converted into heat by, for example, the action of the brakes in a car or train. Energy can be stored in the form called potential energy, for example, a diver standing on a board has potential energy, but when he dives the potential energy becomes kinetic energy. Einstein's theory suggests that mass is also a form of energy.

SI units

The SI unit of force is the newton (N). 1 N of force causes a mass of 1 kg to move with an acceleration of 1 meter per second.

Energy from the sun

The Sun is the source of most of the energy that is used on Earth. It is the original form of energy where it is produced by nuclear fusion. Nuclear energy is another important source of energy.

Light 

Light is a form of energy that travels freely through space. It is electro-magnetic radiation just like radio waves, infrared radiation and x-rays. We can see only part of the range of electro-magnetic radiation. The part we can see is light.

Light from hot objects

Most of the light we see comes originally from very hot objects. The hotter the object, the further towards the blue end of the spectrum is the light that it gives out.

In empty space, light travels at about 300 million metres per second. The light from the Sun takes 8 minutes to reach the Earth.

Sun is the main source of light and energy.

AMAZING FACT !

* Fireflies produce light to attract mates.
* Laser is an abbreviated form of 'Light Amplification by Stimulated Emission of Radiation.

The man behind the discovery

Christiaan Huygens was a Dutch physicist who first suggested that light travels as waves. He invented new ways of making glass lenses for telescopes.

Christiaan Huygens

White light

When white light is passed through a prism it bends at the boundary between the air and glass. Each colour that makes up white light has a different wavelength and bends differently. The red waves bend the least and the violet the most.

White light

The coloured lights at a disco are produced by shining white light through coloured filters.

The white light splits up into its component waves and shows the spectrum of colours known as the visible spectrum. The coloured lights at a disco are produced by shining white light through coloured filters.

The VIBGYOR

During heavy rainfall, when the Sun is behind you. You will see a rainbow. As rays of sunlight pass through raindrops in the sky, the raindrops act like tiny prisms. The white light splits into a spectrum inside the drops and reflects back as an arc of colours.

The seven colours of the rainbow are Violet, Indigo, Blue, Green, Yellow, Orange and Red.

Sound

Sound is a form of wave motion. Sound is produced whenever things move or vibrate. For example, when the skin of a drum is struck with a drumstick it moves to and fro. This movement produces vibrations in air and sets up a sound wave.

Sound ! What is it ?

We are most used to sound waves that travel in the air. We are surrounded by various sounds such as sea tides, thunder, chirping of birds, roar of traffic, loud music etc. All these sounds are the result of vibrations. One can feel sound vibrations. These vibrations are caused by the motion of particles of matter that collide with each other and pass on energy as a travelling wave.

When the phone rings its vibration can be felt by touching it.

Wavelength of sound

Different sound waves have different frequencies and thus have different wavelengths. Two sound waves can also be different because one produces a larger amount of movement in the material than the other. In this case we say that the waves have different amplitudes. How loud a sound is, depends on the amplitude of the sound waves.

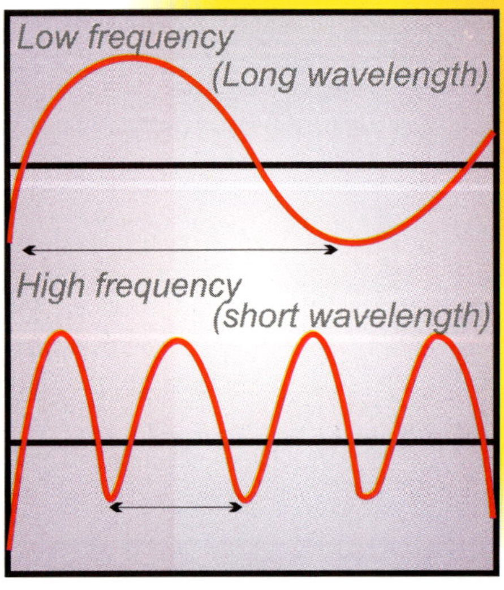

Hearing through Ears

We hear sound through our ears. When sound waves enter our ear the tiny hair in our inner ear each resonate at a particular frequency, so that it responds to sound at that frequency. Young people can hear higher range of frequencies than the old people.

We hear sound through our ears.

Travelling of sound

Sound travels at different speeds in different media; the denser the medium, the faster it travels. For example, sound travels faster through water than through air. The Mach number compares the speed of an object with the speed of sound, travelling through the same media. Some aircraft frequently travel faster than sound and their speeds can be given as a Mach number. Mach 1 is the speed of sound, Mach 2 is twice a speed of sound, etc.

AMAZING FACT !

Dolphins are able to communicate in deep water at very long distances with the help of sonar. This shows that sound travels faster through water than through air.

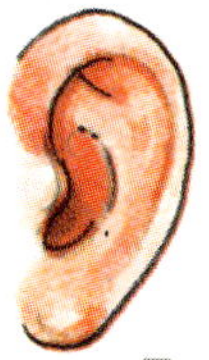
Human Ear

Bat

Cricket

Frog

Animal hearing

Different animals hear at different frequencies. Humans can hear sound at frequencies up to 20 kHz, bats can hear up to 120 kHz, crickets up to 100 kHz and frogs up to 50 kHz.

Magnetism and Electricity 

Magnetism is the force that acts between certain objects at a distance or when they are touching. Electrical processes involve the flow of electric charges, which come in two types, positive and negative.

Magnetism

Magnetism is a special kind of force that is possessed by some objects. Magnets are all around you in your home. Magnets attract iron, nickel, cobalt and most types of steels. There are two types of magnets – permanent magnets and electro-magnets.

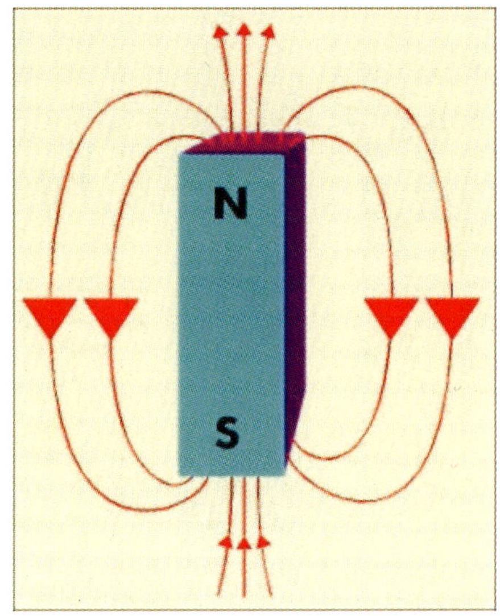

Magnetism – a permanent bar magnet

Poles of the magnet

Magnets exert invisible forces through their poles. The lines of force of the magnetic fields can be seen if iron filings are sprinkled on a paper on the top of the magnets. The iron filings follow the lines of force showing that these are concentrated at magnets' poles.

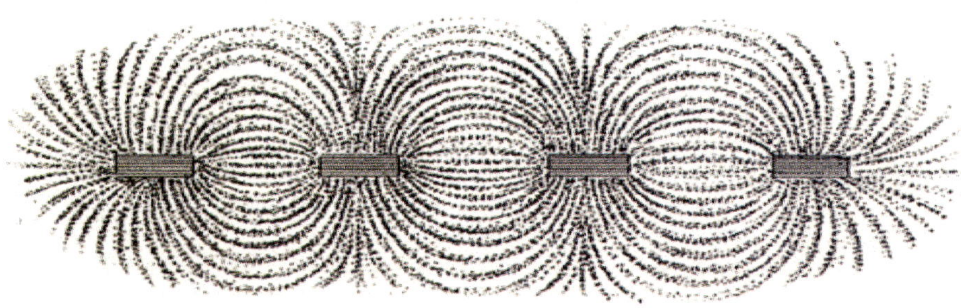

Magnetic fields can be illustrated using magnets and iron filings.

Electricity

Electricity makes cling-film stick to your hands, and sparks jumps through the air. Electricity is the most useful form of energy. Electricity is made up of lots of tiny particles called electrons which lie inside the atoms. The electrons in each atom carry negative charge and nuclei of atoms carry positive charge.

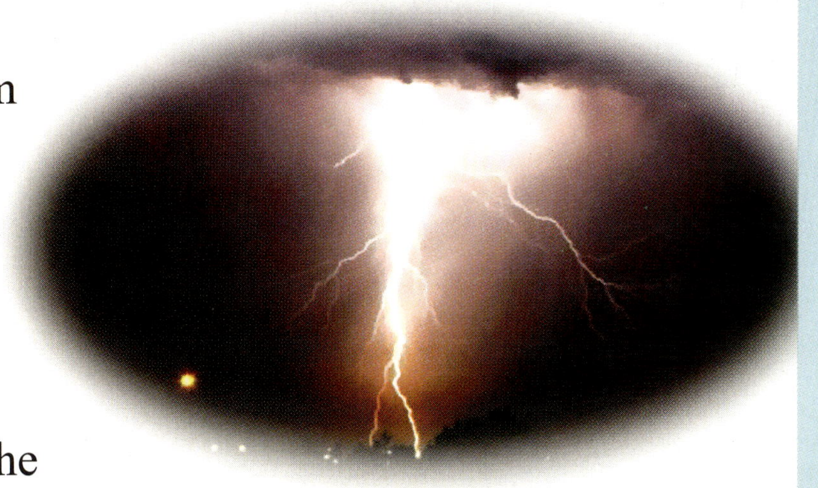

Lighting is a form of electricity that creates an electric current during lightning.

Conductors and insulators

Materials that allow electric current to flow through them are known as conductors. Metals like aluminum and copper are good conductors. Materials that do not allow electric current to pass through them are termed as insulators. Plastic, wood and rubber are few examples of insulators.

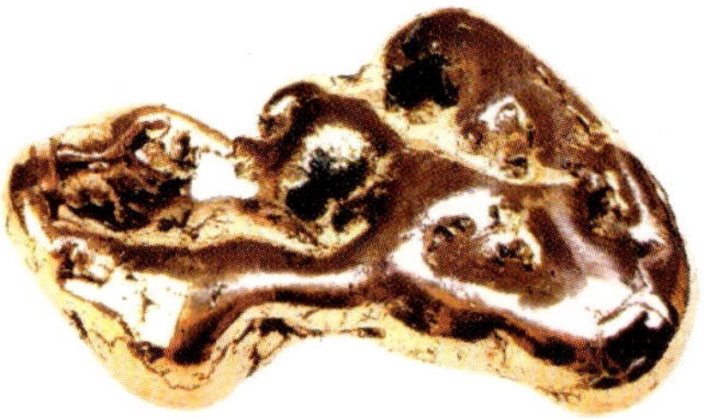

Copper

Wood

AMAZING FACT !

Michael Faraday discovered that a changing magnetic field also produces a current. The electric current producing dynamo, also works on the same principle.

Air and  Atmosphere

Air is a mixture of gases. The layer of air which surrounds the Earth is called the atmosphere. We cannot see or smell air, yet it is as real as the table you are working on. We can feel it moving when the wind blows.

Air

Around 99 per cent of air is composed of the colourless, odourless and tasteless gases that are oxygen and nitrogen. The other gases present in our atmosphere are in very small amount. These gases are, carbon dioxide, neon, sulphur dioxide and carbon monoxide.

Earth is surrounded by a blanket of air known as atmosphere.

Air pressure

Air exerts a pressure on us all the time. In fact, the pressure of air on the Earth's surface is roughly around 1 kg/cm^2; this is the weight of a column of air which is only 1cm by 1cm in area, but 700 km high.

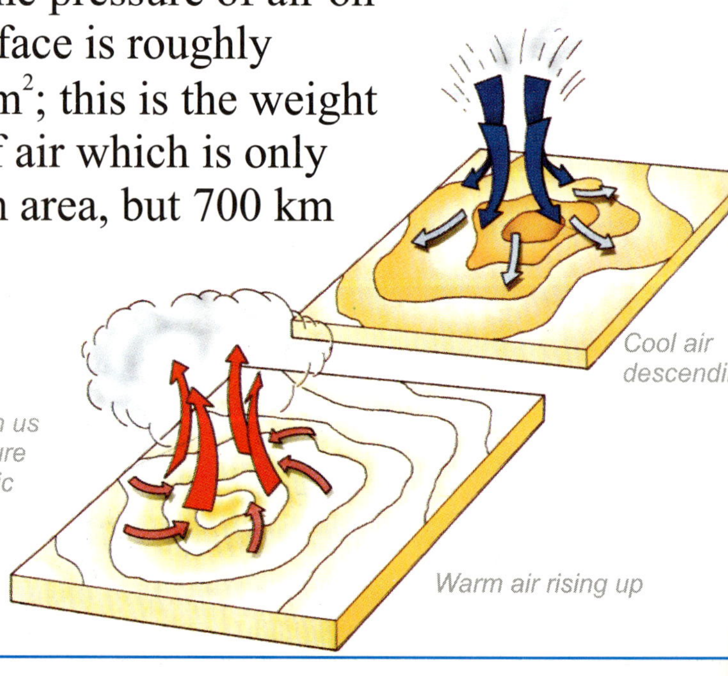

Air exerts a pressure on us all the time. This pressure is known as atmospheric pressure.

Atmosphere

The atmosphere is the band of gas known as air, surrounding the Earth. It extends from the Earth's surface into outer space. It is made up of 78 per cent nitrogen, 21per cent oxygen and 1per cent other gases. It protects us from the harmful rays of the Sun.

AMAZING FACT !

Air is lighter than water, enabling inflatable dinghies to float.

Atmospheric pressure

A bucket full of air weighs about the same as two pages this book. The weight of the air above is always pressing down on us. This force pressing on a given area is called atmospheric pressure. Atmospheric pressure is measured with a barometer.

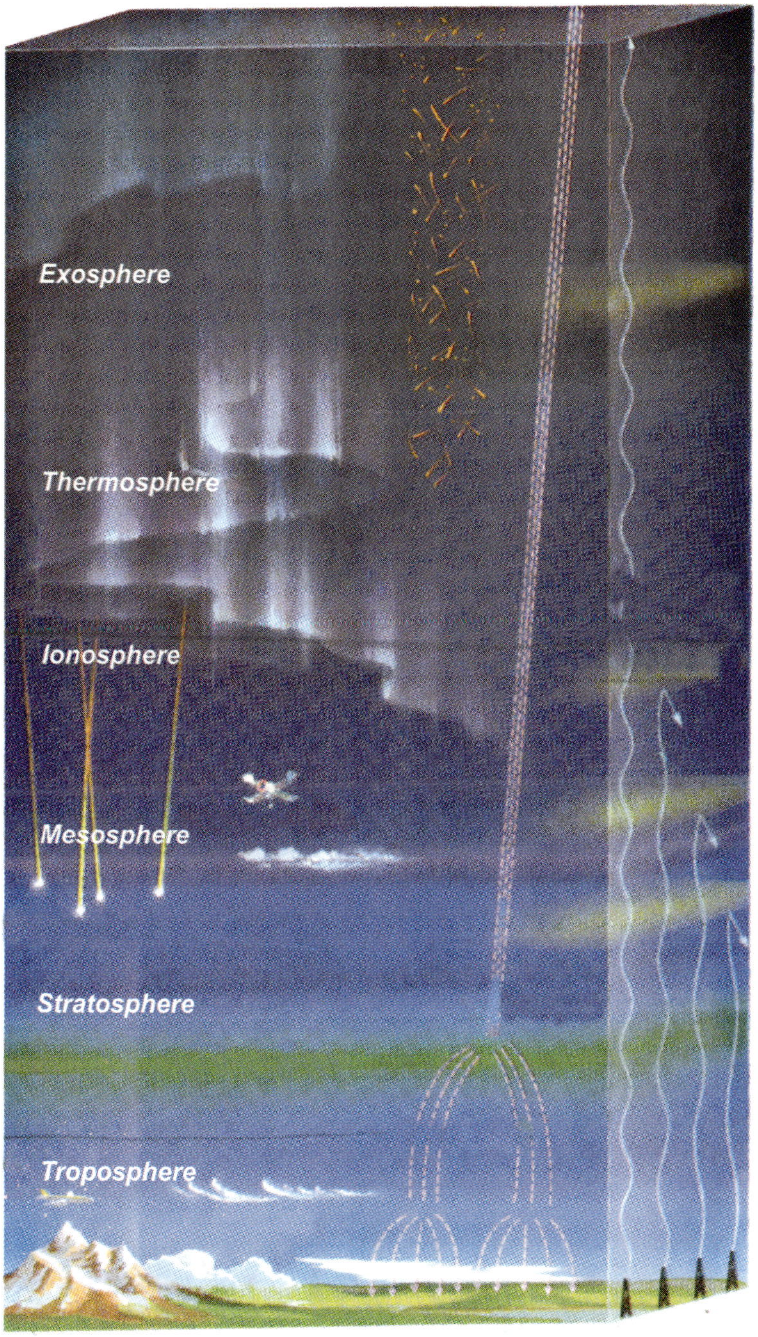

Layers of atmosphere

Water 

Chemically, water is a molecule consisting of two atoms of hydrogen linked with chemical bonds to one atom of oxygen. Water probably has the best known chemical formula : H_2O. It is the most important substance for survival.

Water

Water is a colourless, odourless and tasteless liquid. Water covers about 71per cent of the Earth's surface. A person can live without food for many days but without water, life cannot last more than few hours. The human body consists of 70 per cent water.

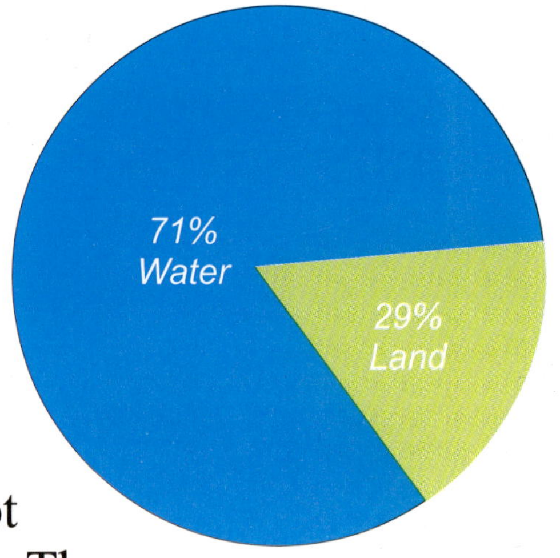

Uses of water

Water is used by all living things in various ways. Plants need water to grow. They usually take water through their roots. They use water and other chemicals to make the substances required for growth. Animals too require water for their survival. Human beings use water in various ways, for example, for drinking, for washing, for bathing, etc.

A boy drinking water.

A lady washing clothes.

A lady cooking food.

Water supplies

The water we use in our homes is rain water from wells or rivers. Before this water can be pumped to our homes it must be cleaned at water works. There first the sand particles are filtered from the water and some of the bacteria are also removed. To clean any remaining bacteria, chlorine gas is bubbled through the water. To prevent tooth decay fluoride is added to it. Eventually this cleaned water is supplied to our homes.

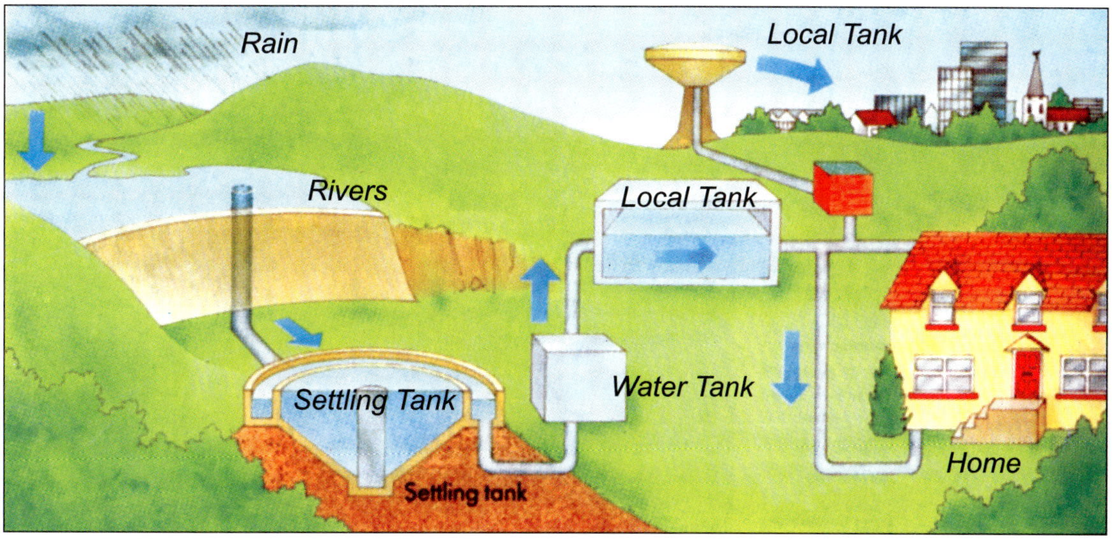

This is the process by which water is supplied to our homes.

From liquid to gas.

From solid to liquid.

Change the state of water

Temperature changes the state of water. At temperatures above 100°C it becomes water vapour or the gas. At 0°C water freezes to form ice. Most solids become denser than their liquid form when they freeze, but water is at its densest at 4°C which is still in a liquid form.

AMAZING FACT !

Deserts have no free water in lakes or streams, rain is very rare in these areas. There are occasional wells and wet places in these areas which are known as oases.

Ecology 

Ecology is the science that studies how plants and animals live together, and how they affect, and are affected by the world around them. Scientists who study ecology are known as ecologists.

Ecology

Ecology is the study of animals and plants in their natural surroundings and how each species fits into its ecosystem. There are many complicated links between plants, animals and their environment. For example, thrushes eat the berries of the trees like the mountain ash. The seeds inside the berries pass through the guts and come out in the thrush's droppings. The seeds grow into new trees which produce more berries. In bad summers, the trees produce few berries and the thrushes cannot feed so many young, so the number of thrushes fall. The trees therefore depend on the thrushes, and thrushes depend on the trees and both are affected by the weather.

Ecology is the everything related to all living organisms. From tiny microbes to giant animals.

Ecologists at work.

Study of ecology

Scientists who study ecology are termed as ecologists. Ecologists try to find out why plants and animals live in some places and not in others and to discover exactly what conditions they need to survive. They also try to discover how much space an animal needs and they study food chains to find out how the plants and animals are linked together.

Living spaces

Ecology also shows how plants and animals depend on all the features that make up their surroundings, called their environment. Rattlesnakes and cacti, for example, are adapted to live in the desert environment, and this is called their habitat. To survive there they must have ways of saving water, keeping cool, coping with the shifting sand and avoiding their enemies. For example, the spines of cactus are there to stop them from being eaten by animals.

AMAZING FACT !

Ecologists recently warned that widespread killing of snakes in Thailand could damage the rice crops. But people ignored it and the number of rats kept growing which eventually resulted in damaging of rice, crops.

Cacti have spines in which they store water.

Cycles in Nature

Nature has provided us with air that comprises several gases such as oxygen, carbon dioxide, nitrogen, etc. Water, as we know is a liquid state of matter that is formed with the combination of hydrogen and oxygen. All these go round in our atmosphere forming cycles.

Oxygen cycle

Oxygen is the major component of living. Every living being needs oxygen for living. It is used again and again in a process termed as the oxygen cycle.

Oxygen Cycle

Animals and humans take in oxygen from the air through their nose. Carbon dioxide released during breathing is taken up by plants which release oxygen back into the air as they breathe.

Nitrogen cycle

Although all humans and animals breathe in nitrogen all the time. The nitrogen that they need enters their bodies in another way, as part of a constant movement of nitrogen called the nitrogen cycle. In this cycle nitrogen moves from the air into plants and animals and back again.

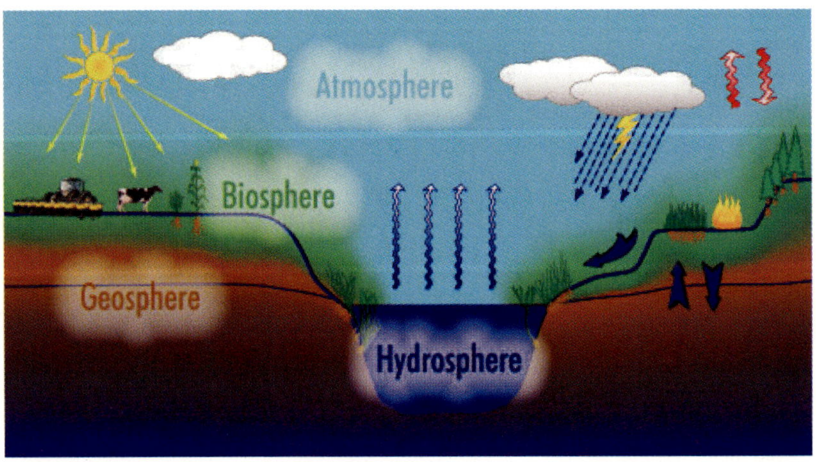

Nitrogen cycle

Water cycle

Water goes round and round in a process termed as the water cycle. In the warmth of the sun, water evaporates from water bodies. The water turns into water vapour, this process is termed as evaporation. The water vapour cools as it rises into the atmosphere. Cool air cannot hold as much water vapour as warm air, so some of the vapour turns into water droplets. This process is termed as condensation. The tiny droplets form clouds, combine to form larger droplets and eventually fall on the land. This rain water again flows to the water bodies and the process repeats again.

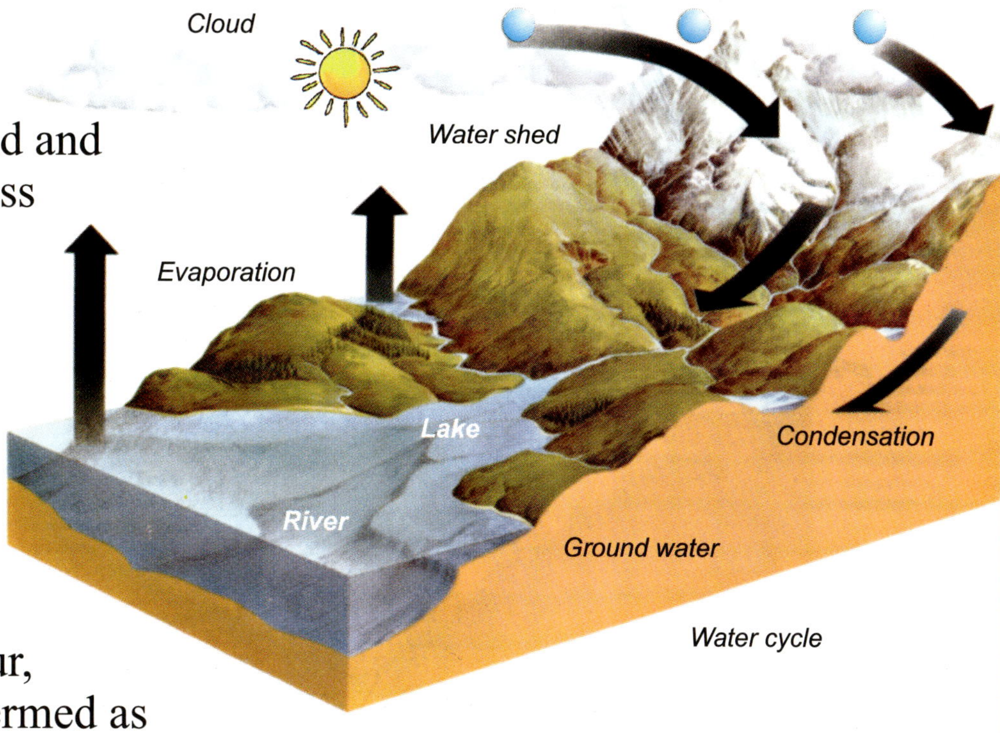

Water cycle

Carbon cycle

Carbon is used again and again in a process called the carbon cycle. Plants take in carbon dioxide from the air through leaves.

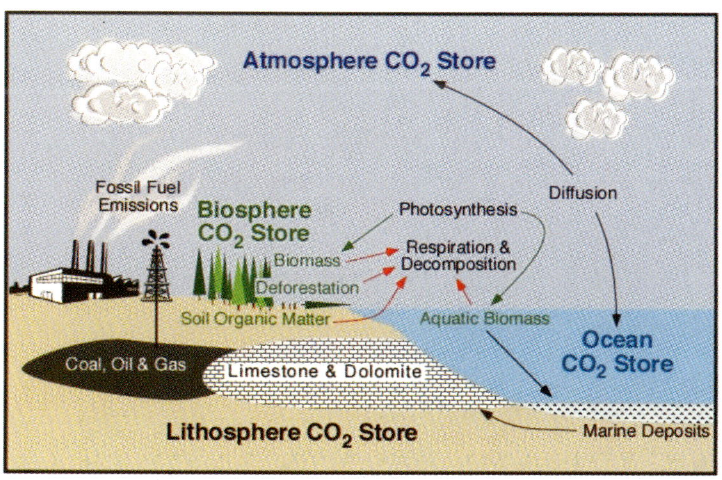

Carbon cycle

AMAZING FACT !

Plants absorb nitrogen compounds from the soil through the roots. These compounds come mainly from the decaying remains of dead plants and animals.

Carbon is then transferred to animals as food who release it back into the air as they breathe.

Producers

Producers are the first link of food chain. Producers are the green plants that range in size from tiny mosses to giant trees. Plants instead of moving around like other living beings grow rooted in the soil or attached to the ground.

Plants

Plants do not feed like animals, although they take chemicals from the soil or from their surroundings to grow. Instead of eating, most make their own food in special 'chemical factories' in their leaves.

Plants are living organisms that make their own food using water, sunlight and minerals.

Photosynthesis

Photosynthesis, which means building with light, is a remarkable process by which green plants make their food. It is a very complex process with several stages, but the end result is that the plants combine water from the soil with carbon dioxide from the air to make glucose sugar. The process takes place only in the light and in the presence of chlorophyll. Chlorophyll absorbs some

Photosynthesis is a process by which green plants make their own food.

of the light falling on it and uses this energy to drive the food making process. The energy passes from stage to stage and finally ends up as glucose, the starting point for cellulose and starch. Oxygen is given off during the process. To keep the process running, the chlorophyll is unchanged and goes on absorbing light.

Plant variety

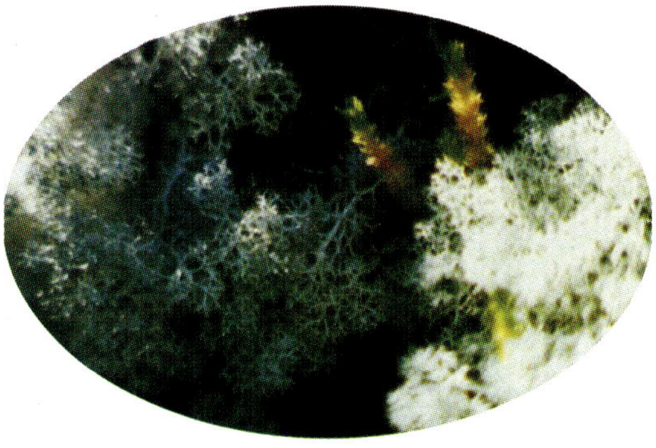

Some plants are not green in colour because of absence of chlorophyll.

We can think of a tree as a 'typical' plant whose roots anchor it in the ground and absorb water and minerals. The main job of its stem or trunk is to hold up the leaves, so they can collect sunshine and carbon dioxide for photosynthesis. Plants are green due to the presence of chlorophyll in them. Some plants are not green, they contain no chlorophyll and cannot photosynthesize. These plants get their food in different ways. There are some groups of living things which are very plant-like, but which scientists do not regard as true plants. Many algae, for example, are made up of a single cell which contains chlorophyll and can photosynthesize. But some algae move about like animals and so algae are generally regarded as a separate group of living things.

AMAZING FACT !

The study of plants is called botany, and people who study them are called botanists.

Plants come in all shapes and sizes, from tiny algae to grasses and giant trees.

Consumers

Consumers are the second link of food chain. Consumers are the animals that live almost everywhere in the world, from polar regions to hot, dry deserts and steamy forests. The biggest weigh over 100 tonnes, the smallest can only be seen through a microscope.

Animals

Animals are one of the five main groups (called kingdoms) into which all living things are divided. It is not always easy to tell animals from plants, but generally animals are able to move about from one place to another and must eat food for their survival.

Animals make the second level of food chain known as consumers.

Eating habits of animals

All animals eat things that have once been alive. Most, such as horses and snails are herbivores and eat plants. Some like tiger and sharks are carnivores, and kill and eat other animals. Some like, human beings and worms, are omnivores and eat almost everything. Others, like vultures and dung beetles are scavengers, and feed on dead and rotten plants and animals.

Herbivores eat green plants.

Carnivores eat flesh.

Vertebrates and invertebrates

The animal kingdom can be divided into two groups: vertebrates and invertebrates. The bodies of vertebrates are supported by the backbone and other bones in skeleton. There are five major groups of vertebrates: fishes, amphibians, reptiles, birds and mammals.

Invertebrates are animals without backbones. These include insects, snails, jelly fishes, squids and worms. Invertebrates do not have bones but may be supported by some kind of hard shell outside or inside their body.

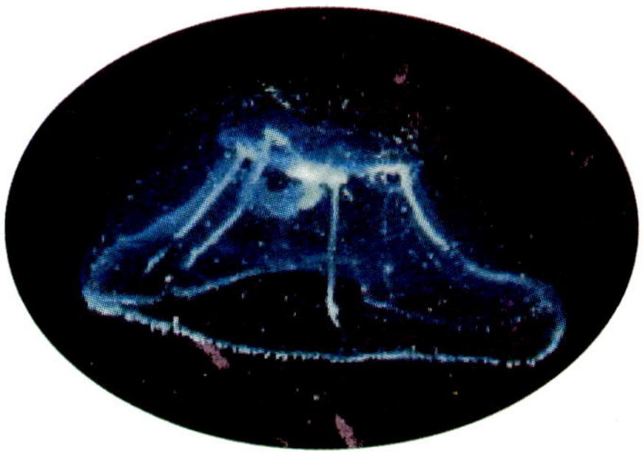

Jelly fish is an invertebrate that does not have a backbone.

Dinosaur is a vertebrate.

Reproduction

Most animals are either male or female and after mating, thc young are born sharing the characteristics of both parents. A small number of animals, such as green fly and water fleas are almost all females and without mating are able to produce female young.

AMAZING FACT !

Some sea anemones are able to divide their own body, splitting off pieces that grow to make the next generation.

Mating Insects

A few like garden snails, are both male and female at the same time, and are able to produce both eggs and sperms. A few like oysters and some fishes change sex at a certain time in their lives or as a result of changes in their environment.

Decomposers

Decomposers are an important link in food chain. Decomposers are the living organisms that are not visible with the naked eyes. A microscope must be used to study them. There are several different groups of micro-organsims: microscopic animals and plants, acteria, viruses and some small fungi.

Micro-organisms

Micro-organisms are very tiny organisms that include bacteria, viruses and fungi. They are also termed as decomposers because they decompose the remains of dead plants and animals that are left over by the consumers.

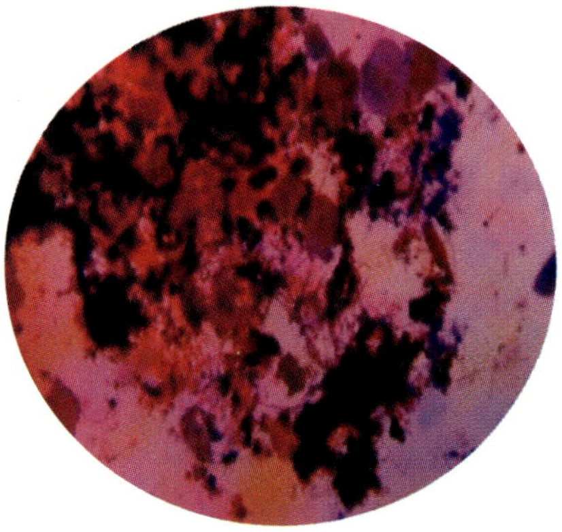

Bacteria are the most ancient and abundant living organisms on Earth.

Bacteria

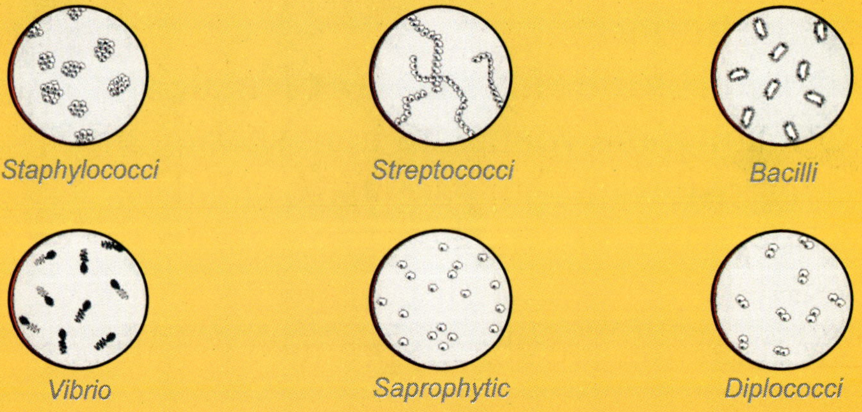

Bacteria are very simple living things, consisting of a single cell. A row of a hundred would just reach across this full stop. Bacteria are found everywhere; in the oceans depths, in soil, or on skins, even floating freely in the air. They are some of the oldest living organisms and fossils have been found of bacteria that lived three thousand million years ago.

A dead, decaying deer.

Bacteria as decomposers

Some bacteria can make their own food by using the Sun's energy (photosynthesis), but most live on decaying plants and animals, or as parasites in other living things. By breaking down dead plants and animals, bacteria return vital nutrients to the soil which are used by plants for growth.

Some fungi grow on dead or dying trees and logs.

Fungi

Fungi are an important group of living things. They get their food by breaking down the tissues of living or dead plants and animals. They can only be seen with a microscope. A few, like mushrooms and toadstools, grow much larger. One vital role of fungi is to decompose dead plants, animals and their waste.

AMAZING FACT !

HELPFUL FUNGI

Yeasts are a type of fungus used in making bread, beer and wine.

Food Chain  and Food Web

All animals depend ultimately on green plants. These plants are known as producers. The next link in the chain are the consumers. To complete the chain are the decomposers who decompose the remains of the dead plants and animals which ultimately result in reproduction of producers.

Food Chain

The plants and animals which live in an area are all linked together by energy and food, forming a food chain. In a garden, caterpillars eat cabbage plant, some of the energy stored in the cabbage is passed to the caterpillars. If a thrush then eats a caterpillar, some of the energy is passed to the thrush. Cabbage, caterpillar and thrush are linked in a food chain.

In this food chain the deer eats the grass, the lion hunts the deer and finally the lion is decomposed and again the same process follows.

Food chains without consumers

In a few food chains, a plant rather than an animal is the consumer. For example, the Venus fly-trap grows in the soil that is short of certain minerals that the plants need to grow. It gets the extra minerals by catching insects in its specially adapted leaves.

Venus fly-trap

Scavengers and decomposers

Scavengers and decomposers are an important part of most food chains. Scavengers include birds such as vultures, animals such as hyenas and some kinds of beetle. They feed on dead plants and animals. Decomposers are certain types of bacteria and fungi which break down remains of dead animals. This puts minerals back into the soil and helps new plants to grow.

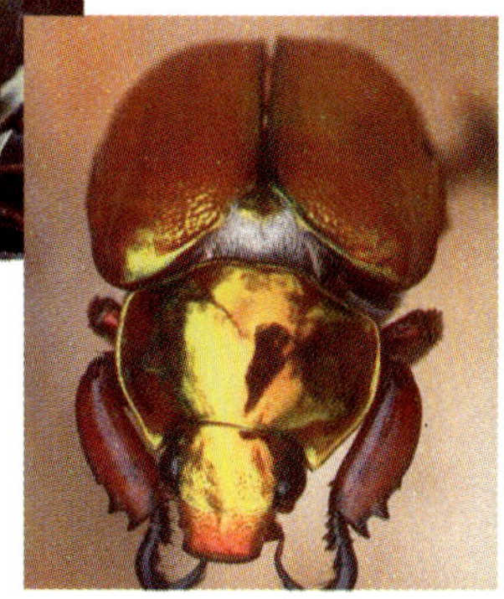

Scavengers and decomposers are essential part of several food chains.

Food webs

In real life, food chains are really not quite so simple. Many different food chains may interconnect to form a food web. The chain in the numbers of animals or plants in one part of food web can affect all the other parts of the web. Human activities often disrupt natural food webs, putting the entire ecosystem out of balance.

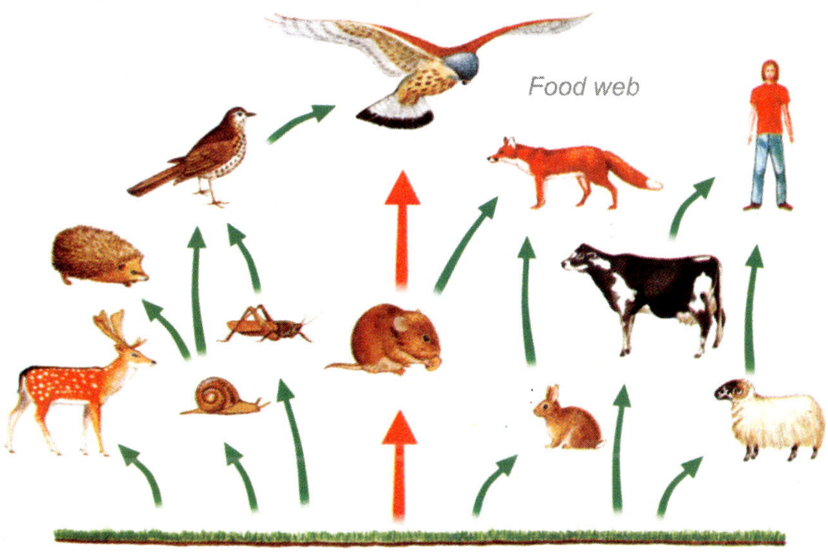

Food web

AMAZING FACT !

The giant panda has to feed for up to 15 hours each day to survive, during which time it consumes up to 20 kg of bamboos.

Our Body 

Like the bodies of all animals, the human body is made up of billions of tiny cells. Particular kinds of cells are grouped together to form tissues and these in turn are organized together into organs such as the heart and the lungs.

Anatomy

Anatomy is the science that deals with the structure of living things. By knowing how organisms are built, we are able to discover and understand how they work. The doctors study the structure of the human body including the skeleton, muscles, blood vessels and nerves as well as all the internal organs so that they know how the body functions in health and illness.

Requirements for survival

Every living organism requires something or the other for its survival. Likewise our body also requires a few essential things for survival as well as proper functioning. These essential things are: water, food and sunlight. There are a few substance that our body uses for energy and growth, they are known as nutrients. There are five types of nutrients: carbohydrates, fats, proteins, vitamins, and minerals.

We get energy to do work from the food we eat.

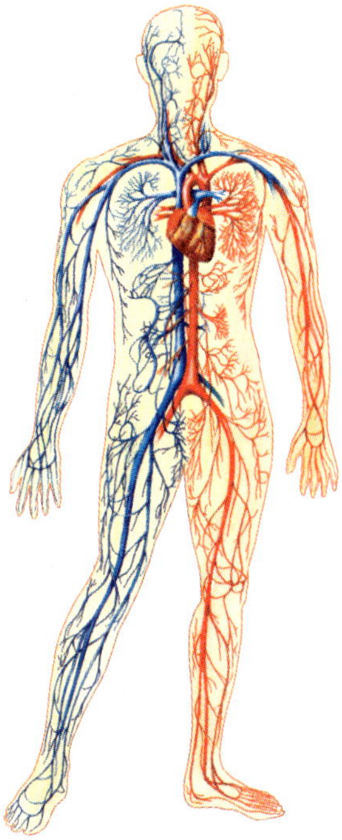

Circulatory System

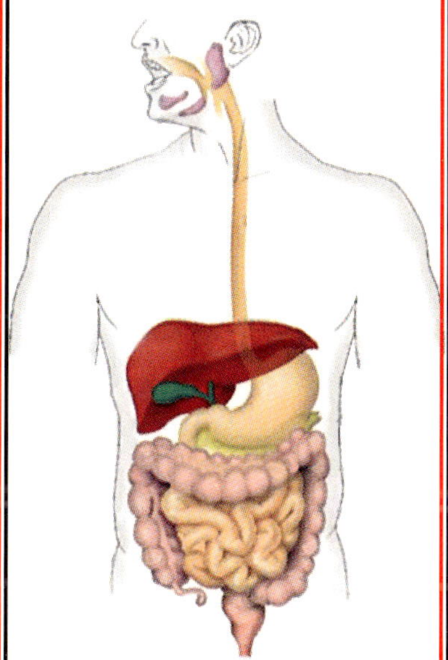

Digestive System

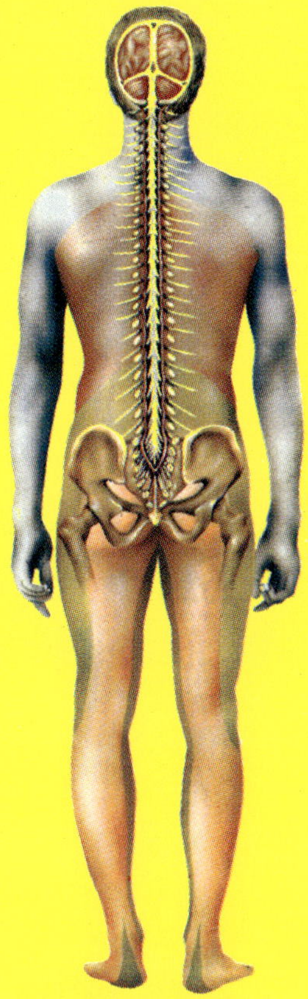

Nervous System

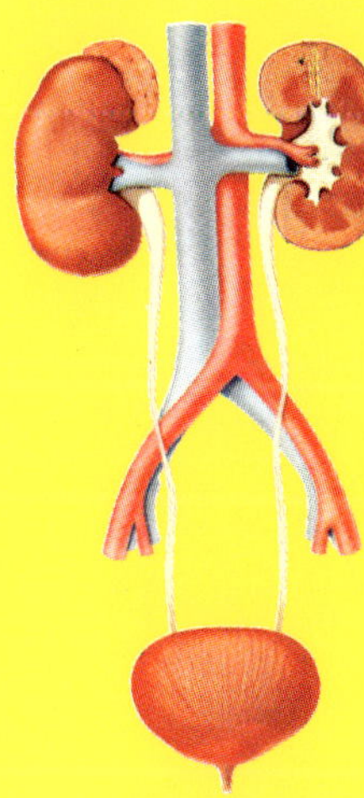

Excretory System

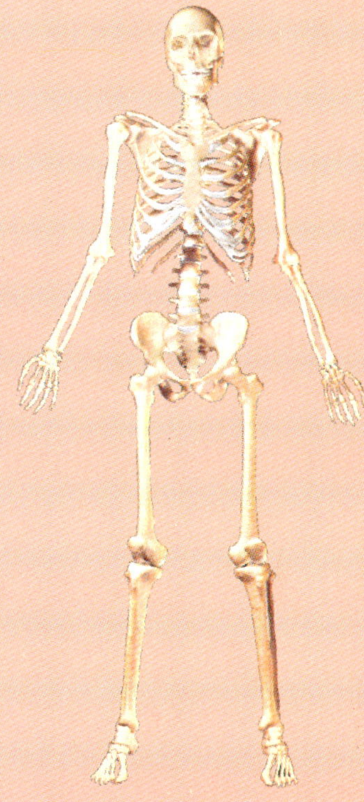

Skeletal System

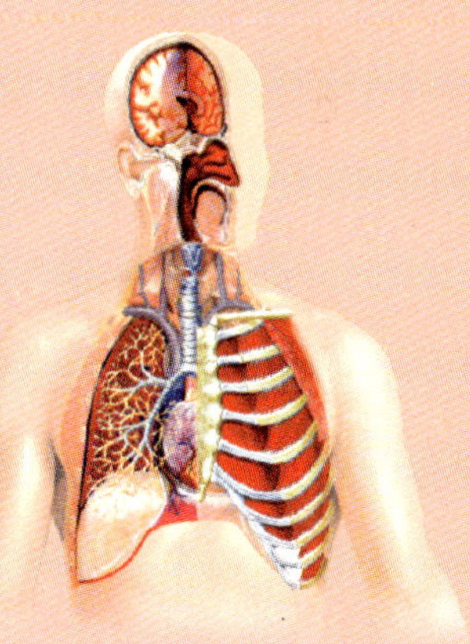

Respiratory System

AMAZING FACT !

More than 200 muscles go into action when you take a step, but only 15 when you smile.

Systems in human body

Our body comprises several systems that perform particular jobs. There are eight main systems in the human body, six of which are shown here.

Sense Organs 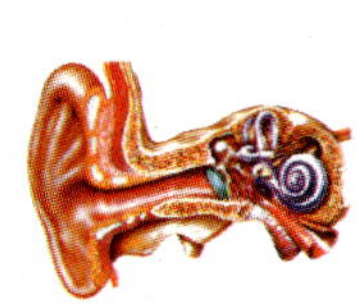

Our senses tell us what is going on around us. Human beings, like all animals, require this information to survive – to move and communicate, to find and escape from danger. Our senses also enable us to enjoy our surroundings.

Sense Organs

People have five main senses: sight, hearing, touch, smell and taste. Each of these senses is located in a part of the body, a sense organ.

Eyes

Eyes are like living cameras. They focus light from the surrounding object to form picture which the brain can understand. At the front of the eye is the clear, round window called cornea behind which is the lens that focuses light on to layer of light-sensitive cells at the back of the eye called retina.

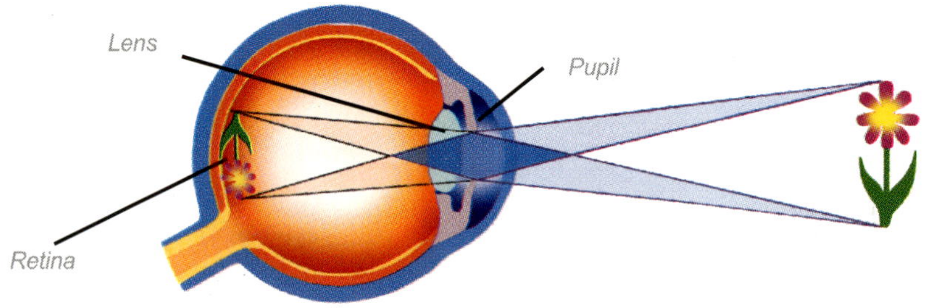

Eye

Ears

We use our ears to detect sound. Sounds make the ear drum vibrate. This makes the tiny bones (ossicle) vibrate, which makes sensory hairs in the inner ear (cochlea) vibrate. These send nerve impulses to the brain when we hear the sound.

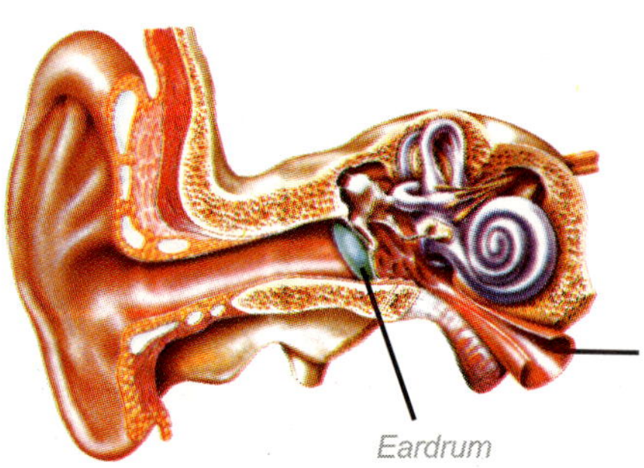

Ear

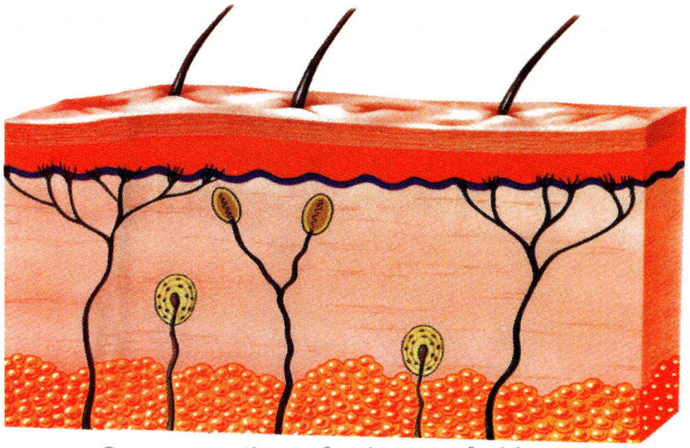

Cross-section of a layer of skin

Skin

Our skin is the protective outer surface which covers the whole of our body. The skin stops the body from losing water, protects it against infection and is an important organ of touch. The outer layer of the skin called the epidermis is made up of dead skin cells. Its cells are constantly being worn away and replaced from below. The layer below is called the dermis. It contains blood vessels, nerves, hair roots and sweat and oil glands.

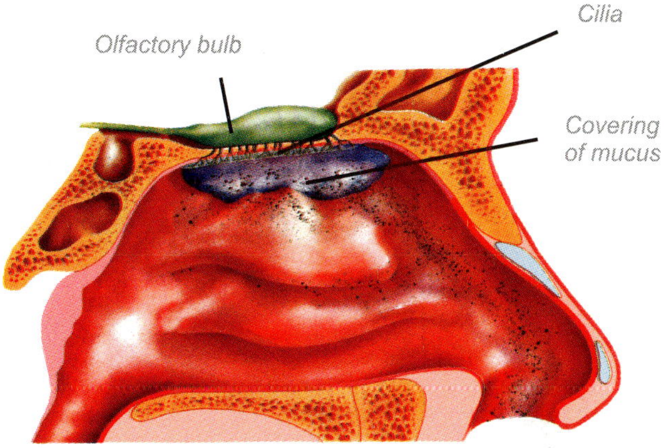

Nose

Nose

The nose enables us to breath as well as smell things. The tubes running from the front of the head into the mouth are called nostrils. The nostrils make up a nose. The olfactory bulb helps us sense smell.

AMAZING FACT !

Human beings can distinguish between 10,000 to 40,000 different odours.

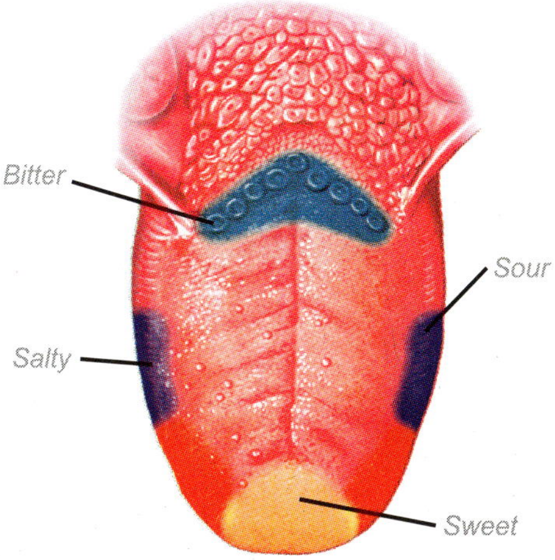

Tongue

Tongue

Taste is one of our five senses. We taste with the help of our tongue. Our tongue has different areas to detect different tastes. The four main flavours that tongue can taste are: sweet, salty, sour and bitter.

Respiration and Digestion

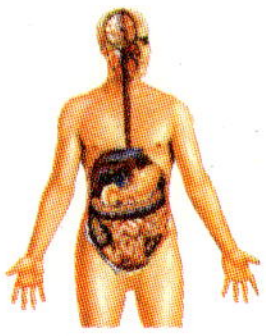

Respiration has two meanings, first breathing, second producing energy from food. All living things respire. Digestion is the process in which animal break down food into simpler substances. These are then absorbed into the blood and carried round the body and are used to build new cells and provide energy.

Respiration

Respiration is the process by which the oxygen we breathe in, reacts with food to release energy. The oxygen passes into the red blood cells through tiny blood vessels in the lungs. The blood then carries the oxygen to every cell in the body where respiration occurs. In these cells, oxygen is combined with sugar and fat in food to release energy some water and the waste gas along with carbon dioxide. The blood then carries the carbon dioxide back to the lungs, from where it is breathed out every time we exhale.

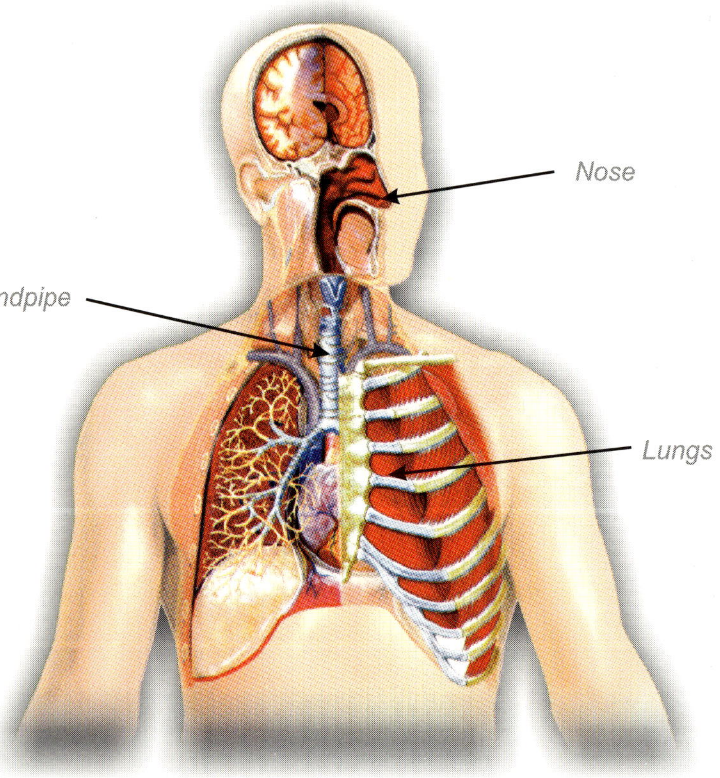

Respiratory System

AMAZING FACT !

The undigested food remains in the colon for 12 to 36 hours. Water and salt are removed from it during this period.

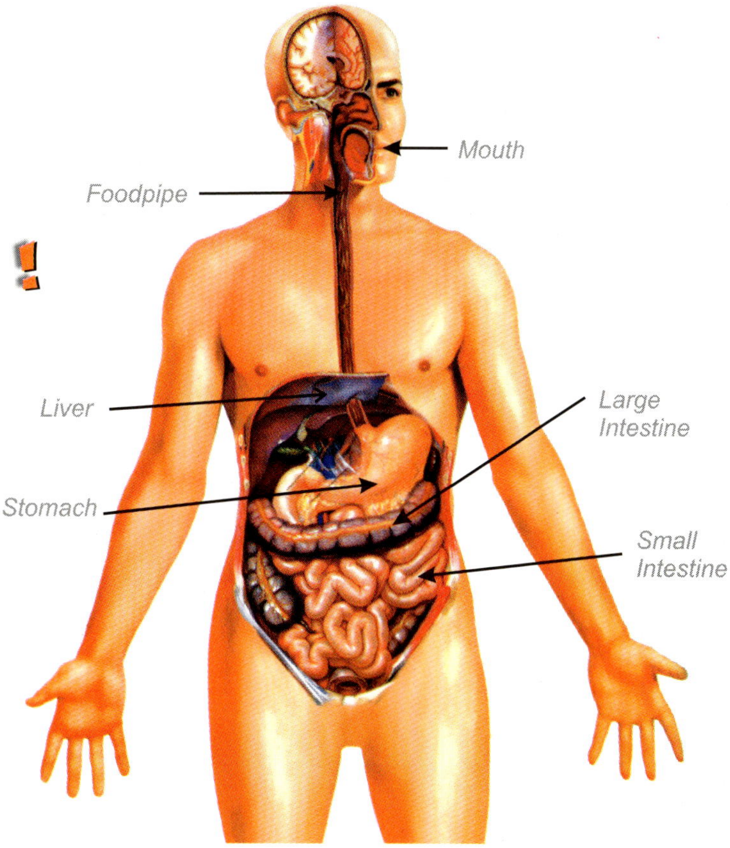

Digestive System

Digestion

You chew your food to break it into small pieces which are easy to swallow. The teeth bite off and chunk the food, then the tongue pushes it to the back teeth which grind it up and mix it with saliva. Saliva softens the food and begins to digest it. You chew the food and finally swallow it. The chewed food passes down your gullet (oesophagus) into your stomach. Muscles in the gullet push it forward by squeezing together behind it and relaxing in front of it in a movement called peristalsis. Then the food goes to the stomach in which the food is mixed with acid and digestive juices called enzymes which can kill any bacteria and help to break the food down. From stomach the food moves to small intestine where the digestion continues. Pancreas break the food down into small molecules. The undigested food passes into the rectum and comes out of the anus as stool.

Nervous and Muscular System

The nervous system of humans and other vertebrates is made up of the brain, the spinal cord and a network of nerves. It is body's communication and control system. All animal movements are controlled by muscles, which work by pulling against the skeleton. Muscles are made-up of fibres.

Nervous System

The nervous system ensures that all the parts of an animal's body are co-ordinated and that the animal responds to any changes to its surroundings. The brain and spinal cord make up the central nervous system. The peripheral nervous system is made up of the nerves that connect all the parts of the body with the brain and the spinal cord.

The nerves carry electrical messages (nerve impulses). There are two types of nerve: sensory nerves that carry information from the sense organ to the brain, the second are the motor nerves through which the brain sends out nerve impulses to the part of the body where action is required.

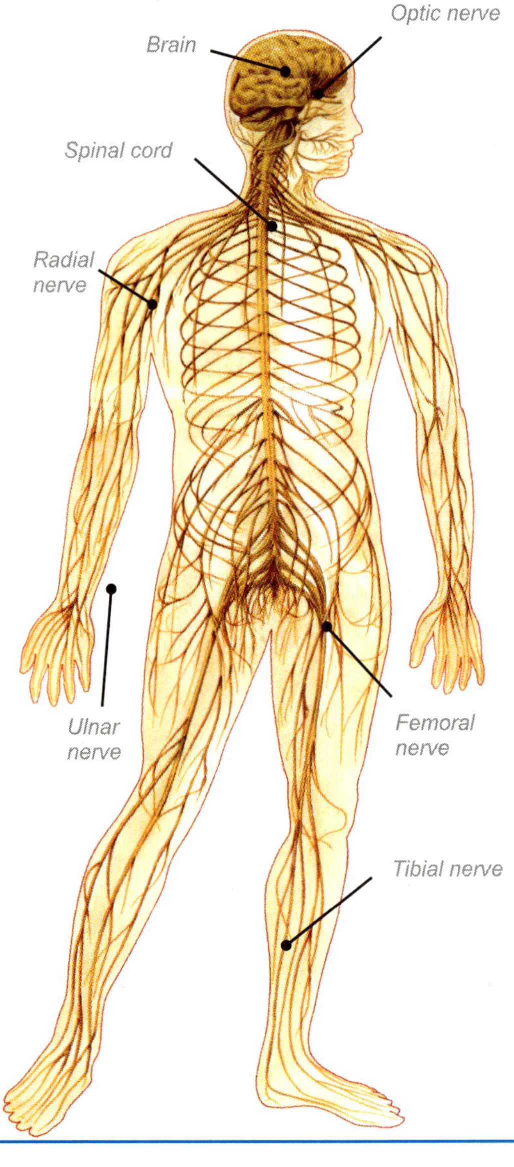

Muscular system

Muscles are made up of muscles cells and are controlled by nerves signals from the brain. They work by contracting. Muscles cannot lengthen themselves but they can be stretched when other muscles pull at them. There are around 650 muscles in our body. Muscles are of three types. The first are the voluntary muscles. These muscles are attached to the bones and are used to move the body. The second type of muscle are involuntary muscles. These muscles can contract without you thinking about it. For example, the muscle around the gut which pushes food along. The third type of muscle is found in the heart. They are termed as cardiac muscles which pump blood around the body.

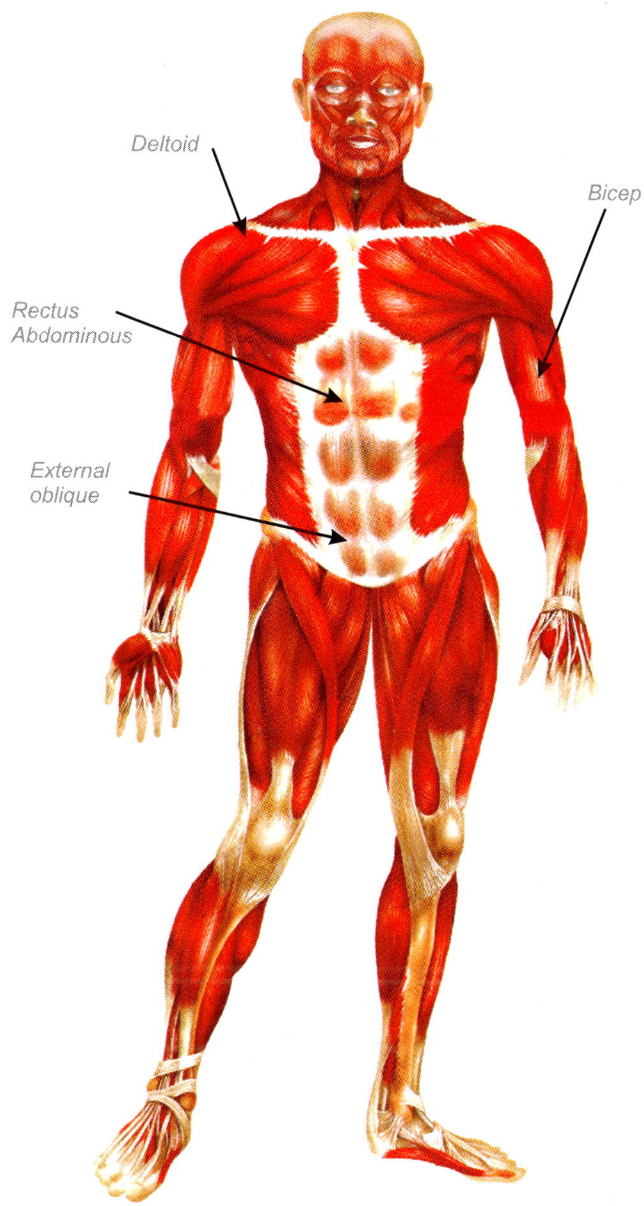

AMAZING FACT !

Pain is an unpleasant feeling that warns us of damage to our bodies.

Skeleton and Bones

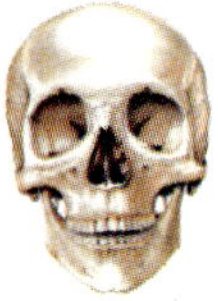

Skeleton is the frame of bones that supports our body. It gives us our shape and enables us to make distinct movements. Bones are the hard parts of our body. They form our skeleton, the frame around which our body is built.

Skeletal System

The skeleton is the frame work of a body, providing support and protection. Our skeleton is joined to allow the muscles to move arms, legs and other parts of our body. Like human all vertebrates have a skeleton. The skeleton is made up of bone and a softer gristly substance called cartilage. The skull and backbone support and protect the central parts of the nervous system, the brain and spinal cord. Attached to the backbone are the ribs, this rib-cage protects the heart, guts and the lungs. The shoulder and hip are the bony connection between the backbone and the limbs. At the bottom end comes the legs and feet.

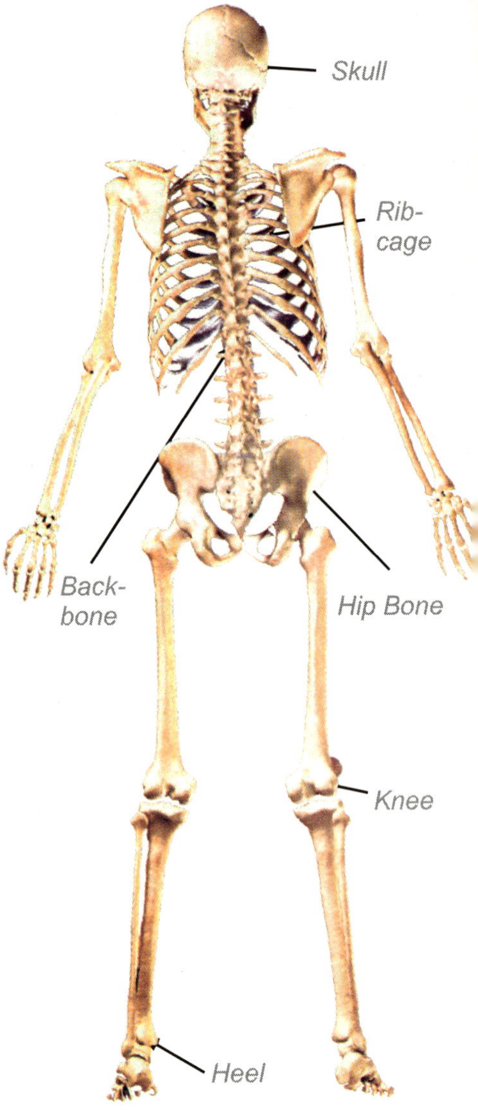

Back of Skeletal System

AMAZING FACT !

Adults have 206 bones in their bodies. Children have more but some fuse together as they grow.

Bones

Bones give us our shape and enable us to move. Bones contain living cells and can regrow if they break. They are as strong as some kinds of steel, but only one-fifth as heavy.

Bones are made out of a mixture of a tough protein called collagen, and very tiny, hard mineral crystals which contain calcium and phosphorus. This mixture gives bones their strength. At the centre of many bones is a soft tissue called bone marrow. This contains blood vessels that supply the bone with food and oxygen. The marrow is also the place where new blood cells continually are made.

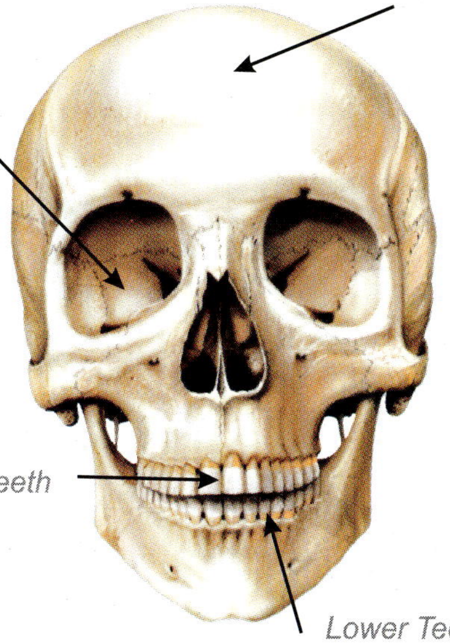

Human Skull

Joints

Joints are the bending and sliding places where bones meet. The bones at joints are covered in smooth cartilage, lubricated by joint fluid, which allows them to move over each other easily. Different types of joint allow different types of movement. Hinge joints, such as the elbow and the knee, allow movements in two directions only. Where greater flexibility is needed, as in the shoulder and hip, ball-and-socket joints are found.

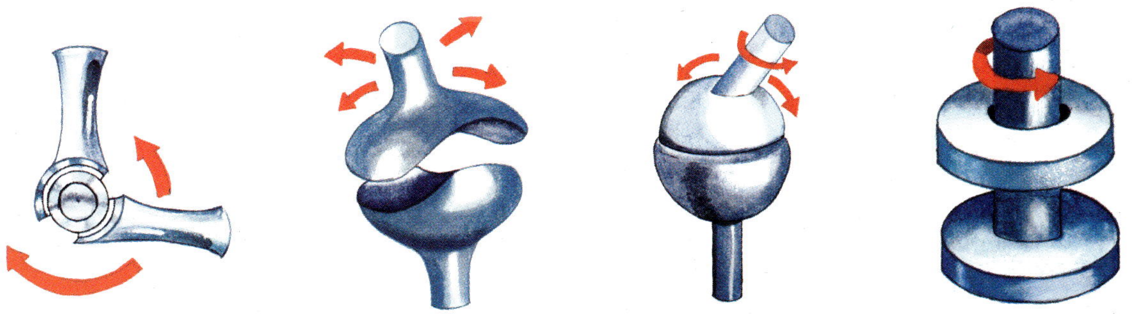
Hinge Joint   Saddle Joint   Ball and Socket Joint   Swivel Joint

Excretion and Reproduction

When chemical reactions take place in any living organism some unwanted waste products are produced. If these build up, they would harm the organism, so the waste materials are excreted.

Excretion

In animals, the most common waste products are water, carbon dioxide and urea, which is produced by the breakdown of protein. These materials pass into the blood. Carbon dioxide is breathed out from the lungs, together with some water vapour. Most of human liquid waste is excreted by the kidneys, in the form of urine. Water and urea are extracted from the blood through a web of tiny blood vessels and tubes. Some valuable substances also leak out, and these, together with 99per cent of the water are re-absorbed before the urine leaves the kidneys. The urine travels to the bladder, from where it is passed out of the body.

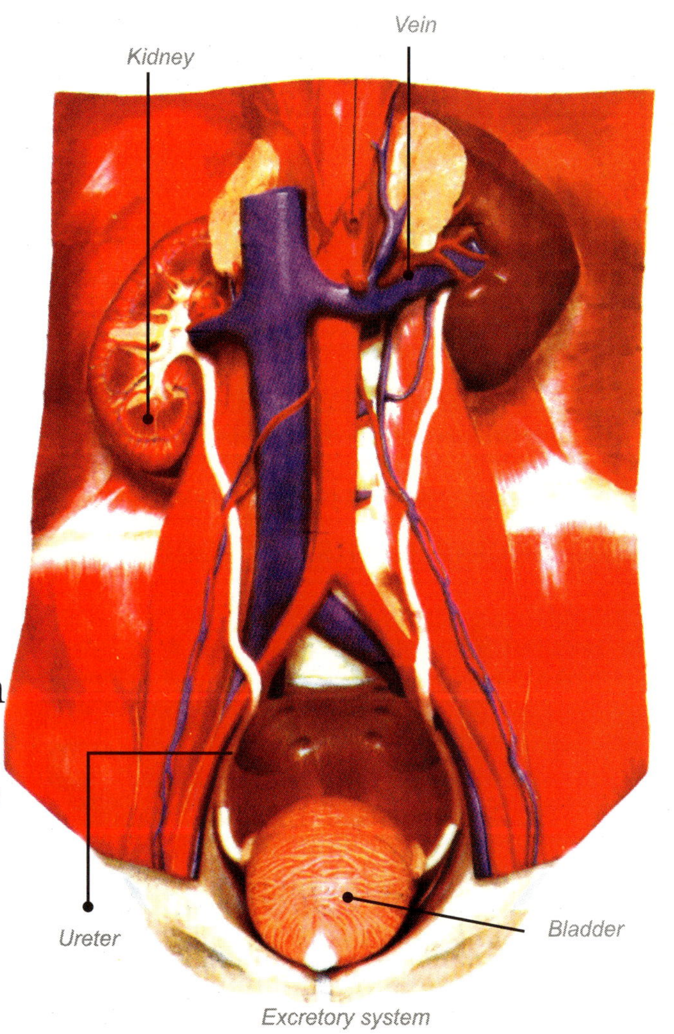

Excretory system

Reproduction

As with most other animals, male and female human beings have different sexual organs (genitals). A man has a penis. Below and behind the penis is a bag called a scrotum, containing two testes.

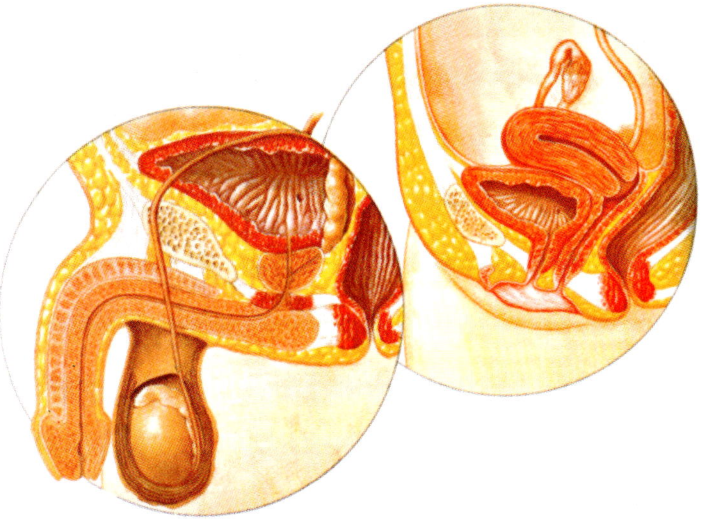

Reproductive systems of male and female.

The opening in a woman's body leading to her reproductive organs is called the vulva. It is surrounded by two thick folds of skin that protect the clitoris, a small bit of sensitive tissue. A channel called the vagina goes from the vulva to the womb (uterus).

AMAZING FACT !

Around the world, about 140 children are born every minute.

A mother nursing her newborn baby.

Two tubes link the womb to the egg-producing ovaries. The sperms of male swim into the woman's womb and up towards her ovaries. If a sperm fertilizes an egg, the woman becomes pregnant.

Heart

The heart is a muscular organ that pumps blood around the body. All vertebrates (animals with backbones) have hearts, as do many larger invertebrates, including earthworms, crabs, insects, snails and squids.

Heart

In humans, the heart is in the middle of the chest. It is made up of four muscular chambers: two atria and two ventricles. Their strong contractions as they pump the blood are our heartbeats. The pulse is a wave of blood being pushed by a heartbeat along a blood vessel (tube) running from the heart. These blood vessels are close to the surface at the wrist and neck, which are the best places to feel your pulse. Measuring your pulse rate tells you how fast your heart is beating. A normal rate is about 65-85 beats per minute for an adult.

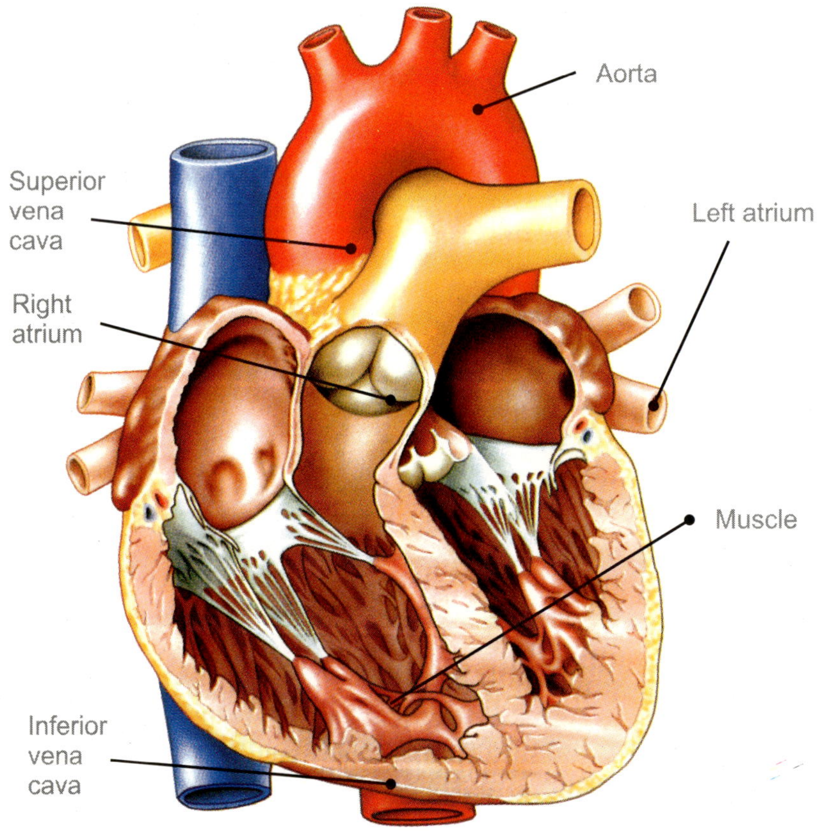

The Human heart

Working of heart

The left side of the heart takes in oxygen-carrying blood from the lungs. It then pushes it out along thick-walled bleed vessels called arteries into very thin blood vessels called capillaries. The capillaries carry the blood to and from all parts of the body before joining up with thin-walled blood vessels called veins. The veins carry the blood, which now contains the waste gas carbon dioxide, back to the right side of the heart and the circulation begins again. The heart pushes the blood with the waste carbon dioxide out to the lungs and the gas is breathed out when you exhale.

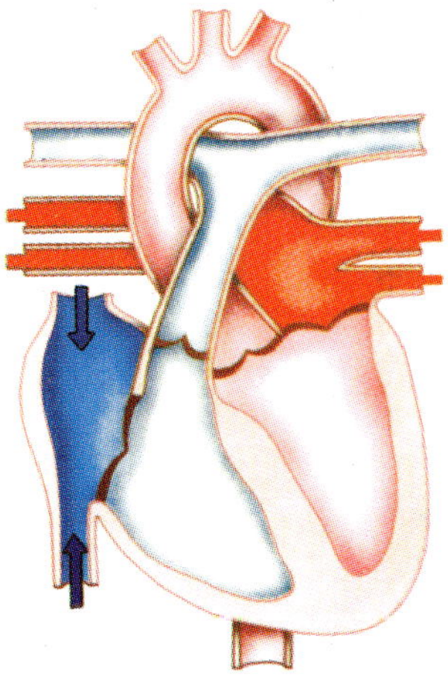

Blood floods into relaxed atria

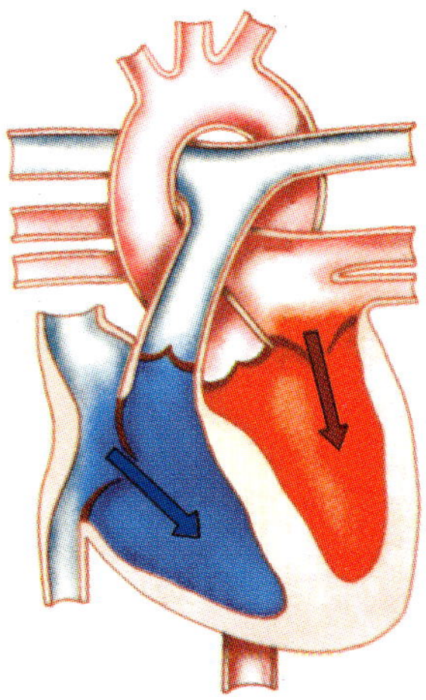

The contraction squeezes the arteria, driving blood into ventricles

AMAZING FACT !

Animal blood is not always red. Different blood pigments have different colours. Hemoglobin is the most common. Hemocyanin is bluish and is found in some invertebrates.

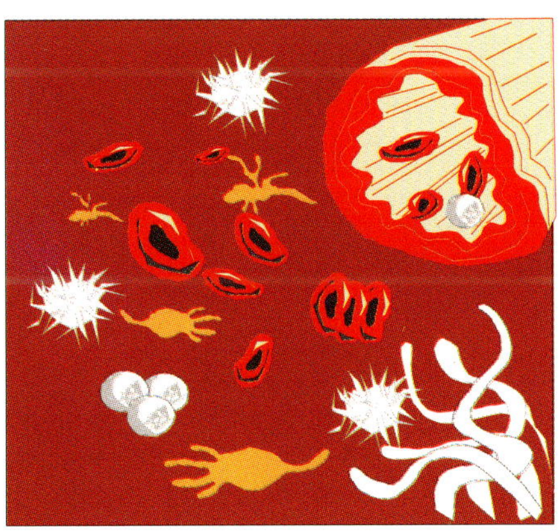

Our blood comprises four elements : red blood cells, white blood cells, platelets, and plasma.

Blood

Blood is the vital life-sustaining liquid that is found in the bodies of all large animals. It is pumped round the body by the heart through a network of arteries, veins and capillaries. The kidneys control the amount of water in the blood and expel, as urine, the waste products of the body. The blood carries oxygen and food materials from the digestive system to the body tissues.

Energy  from Food

Our body depends on energy, as do our homes, vehicles and factories on earth. The sun is the source of nearly all our energy. Without energy nothing would live, move or change.

Energy

Energy is the basic requirement for us that enables us to do work. We get energy from the food we eat. The food may be from plants or from animals that feed on plants. The range of foods that we eat most of the time is called our diet.

Our diet should provide all the things that our body needs for growth, repair and health. Sometimes people change their diet for health reasons. It may be to lose weight, to control a disease, or to prepare for sporting events.

Salads are rich source of vitamins and proteins

Healthy diet

A healthy diet is one that provides the right nutrients (nourishing food substances) in the right amounts. A diet that includes plenty of cereals, fruit and vegetables.

It provides a good balance of nutrients. A diet that is mostly made up of chips, sweets and salty snacks is much less healthy, because it is unbalanced. It contains too much fat, sugar and salt, and not enough protein and vitamins.

Food for energy

The smallest amount of energy that you need to stay alive is called your basal metabolic rate (BMR). The average adult BMR is between 6000 and 7000 kilojoules a day (a kilojoule is a unit for measuring energy). The amount of energy you need on top of your BMR, when you wake up and start moving, depends on your age, your sex and how energetic a job or activity you are doing – a young athlete uses far more energy than an elderly person.

Types of food

Meat and fish : Mostly protein with some fat and oil. Many vitamins, especially in fish oil.

Eggs and diary produce : Mostly fat, especially butter and cheese. Eggs have a lot of protein and many vitamins.

Cereals : Mostly starchy carbohydrates with a little protein. Some vitamins.

Vegetables : Contain a lot of water, some carbohydrate and protein. Very little fat. Very rich in vitamins and minerals.

Fruits : Contain a lot of water with some carbohydrate and a little protein. Rich in vitamin C.

Sweets and cakes : Mostly carbohydrates, especially sugar, with some fat and a little protein. No vitamins.

AMAZING FACT !

The amount of calories we take depend on weight, metabolism.

- Our Universe
- Stars and Galaxies
- Milky Way
- Constellations
- Sun
- Mercury
- Venus
- Earth
- Moon
- Mars
- Asteroids
- Jupiter
- Saturn
- Uranus
- Neptune
- Pluto
- Comets
- Meteors and Meteorites
- Astronomy
- Space Exploration

Unit-2

Up Above

Our Universe

The Universe refers to everything that exists, from the Earth to the most distant parts of space. The Universe comprises countless galaxies of stars. The farthest ones we can see are so distant that their light takes billions of years to reach us.

Beginning of the Universe

Scientists believe that the Universe started about 15,000 million years ago. It began with an explosion that they call the Big Bang. This was an explosion in which all the matter and energy in the Universe were created. It was the beginning of time and space.

The Universe came into being millions of years ago with an explosion called the Big Bang.

Initial stages

Initially, the Universe was very hot and dense. It remained so for thousands of years. After three hundred thousand years when the Universe became much cooler; matter, light and other kinds of radiations spread out as space continued to expand. Giant clouds of gases started to collapse on themselves about a million years later. Each of these clouds became a galaxy in which the stars originated.

The never ending expanse of the Universe

Is the Universe still expanding ?

The Universe is still expanding, and the galaxies are moving further and further away from each other. If the Universe continues expanding, thousands of millions of years later the stars will run out of fuel and finally they will stop glowing.

AMAZING FACT !

In the year 1929, Edwin Hubble, an American astronomer showed that the galaxies are moving away from each other and the Universe is expanding. This discovery was termed as Hubble's Law. This law forms the basis of the Big Bang theory.

Scientists believe that the Universe is still expanding.

Stars and Galaxies

Stars are the shining globes of gas. Their heat comes from deep inside, where hydrogen is turned into helium, giving out nuclear energy. When the hydrogen present in a star is exhausted, it eventually dies. Galaxies are the assembly of millions of stars.

Studying stars

By studying many stars, astronomers have found that they belong to different groups. Some are very hot and shine with bluish light, while others are much cooler and look reddish. These tints can be seen in many of the naked-eye stars that form the constellations. For example, the brightest star in the sky, Sirius, is much whiter and hotter than the Sun, while the closest known star after our Sun, Proxima Centauri is small, dim and red, the Sun is a medium hot star.

Cluster of galaxies

Lifespan of a star

Stars do not live forever. Eventually the hydrogen gas fuel in their core is used up. When this happens, the star changes into a new form and finally dies.

AMAZING FACT !

A quasar (quasi-stellar radio source) is something that sends out radio waves and looks like (but is not) a star.

Birth of a star

Stars are born and may shine for thousands of millions of years before they die. A cloud of gas and dust condenses to form a young star. Some massive stars, at the end of their life, explode as supernovae and could become black holes or neutron stars. Smaller stars at the end of their life, expand into red giants and then shrink into white dwarfs that shine dimly.

Galaxies

Our Sun and all the stars you can see in the night sky belong to a giant family of stars that we call the Galaxy. It contains around 100,000 million stars. This Galaxy is known as the Milky Way. Beyond the Galaxy, there are countless other galaxies scattered all across the space.

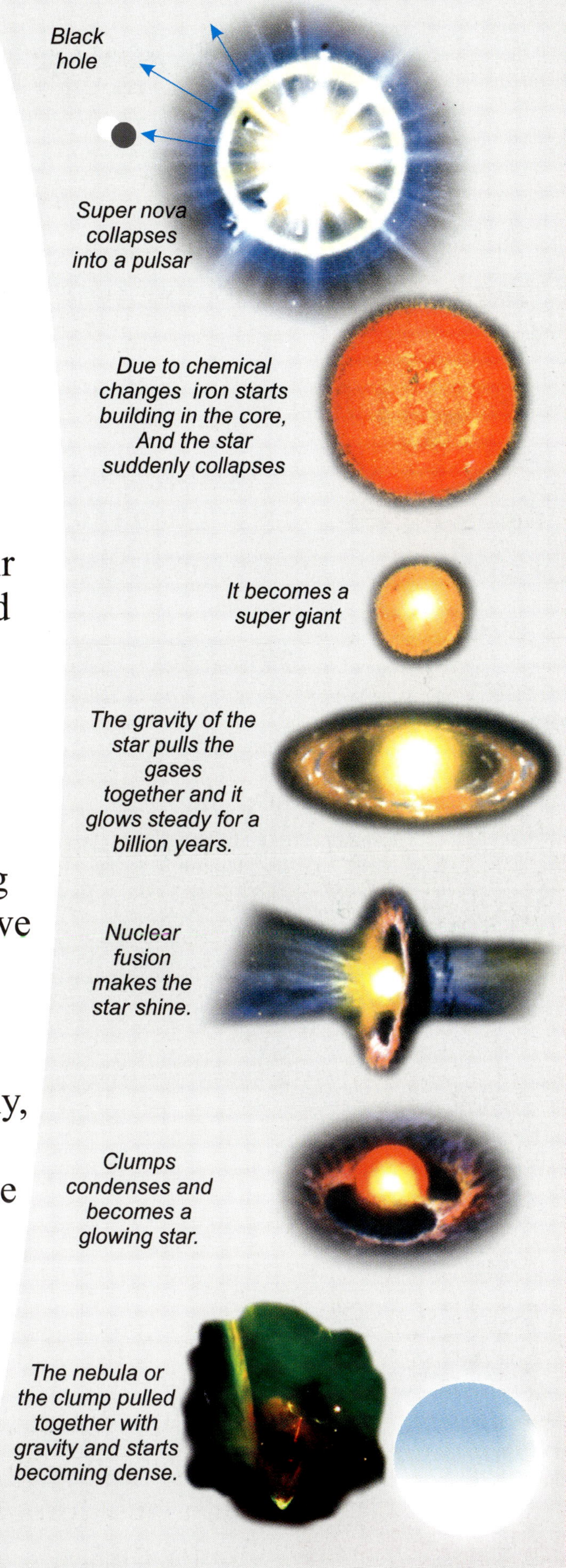

Milky Way is a huge spiral-shaped galaxy of stars.

Milky Way

The Milky Way is the Galaxy that contains our solar system. Our galaxy probably originated soon after the Universe was formed, about 15,000 million years ago. The Milky Way circles the whole sky. We can see parts of it in the night wherever we are on the Earth.

The area of Milky Way

The diameter of the Milky Way is around 1,00,000 light years. It circles the whole sky which one can see wherever one is on the Earth. In the North, the constellations (groups of stars) it goes through include Auriga, Cassiopeia and Cygnus. Dark patches in the Milky Way are actually clouds of dust cutting out the light from the stars. The most famous one, 'the Coalsack', is in the Southern Cross.

The Milky Way measures about 1,00,000 light years across

Origin of our Galaxy

The Milky Way probably began forming soon after the Universe was formed, around 15,000 million years ago. To begin with it may have been a cloud of hydrogen gas. At the centre, where the gas was densest, stars began to form, 'first generation' stars that have formed long ago and died away. Some of these stars exploded as supernovae, throwing out all the new elements such as carbon and iron.

Present state of the Milky Way

The Milky Way galaxy has long spiral arms made up of clouds of material and new stars. Our Sun and the Solar System were born in one of the arms. Every few hundred million years, as the Milky Way spins, the Sun also goes round the centre of the galaxy. There is enough material in the arms for many generations of stars.

AMAZING FACT !

The thickness of the Milky Way at the centre is around 15,000 light years. The speed at which the galaxy rotates is once every 225 million years.

Top view of the Milky Way

Views of the Milky Way

The Milky Way is a spiral galaxy with a nucleus of old stars surrounded by a halo of much younger stars. The name given to the galaxy is because of its appearance like bright, creamy band of stars stretching across the sky when seen from the Earth.

Side view of the Milky Way

Constellations

People usually think of a constellation as a group of stars, such as the seven bright stars of Ursa Major (the Great Bear). It is actually one area of the sky arbitrarily named by astronomers, that fit together to make up the whole sky.

Constellations

Groups of stars that make patterns in certain part of the sky are known as constellations. Some of them were named by the Greeks 2000 years ago, and Arab and Chinese astronomers had their own constellations too. There are 88 constellations and they cover the whole sky. They were probably invented as a way of referring to particular stars. Although the stars in a constellation appear to us to be in a group, they are really vast distances away from each other.

AMAZING FACT !

Many of the old names of constellations are of animals, like Leo (the lion) and Cygnus (the swan).

Orion

Ursa Major

Sagittarius

The constellations you can see at any one point of time vary according to the season, the time of night and where you are on the Earth.

The Zodiac

We cannot see the stars during the day because the Sun is too bright, but if we could we would notice the Sun slowly moving through the star patterns. It makes a trip right round the sky once a year, travelling through a band of constellations called the zodiac.

The ancient Greeks divided the zodiac into 12 equal zones, called the 'signs' of the zodiac.

Each sign corresponds roughly to one of the zodiac constellations, though the official constellations that astronomers use are not all equal in size. People called astrologers make predictions about people's lives, based on the signs of the zodiac.

How were the constellations named?

Many of the constellations were named before 2000 BC by Babylonian astronomers. The oldest are the 12 forming the zodiac. Towards AD 150, when the Greek astronomer Ptolemy published his famous star catalogue, he listed 48. No more were added until explorers began to sail South and saw parts of the sky invisible from Europe and the Mediterranean. The total number is now 88.

Sun

The Sun is a globe of gas, mostly hydrogen, measuring 1,392 thousand kilometres across, over a hundred times the diameter of the Earth. It is the centre of the Solar System and gives the Earth and other planets light and heat.

The Solar System

The word 'solar' means 'to do with the Sun'. It comes from sol, the Latin word for Sun. The Sun and all the things in orbit around it make up the Solar System. It comprises a family of nine planets, most of which have one or more moons. Lots of other smaller objects, such as asteroids (minor planets) and comets, also travel around the Sun. The Sun, which is a star, is by far the largest body in the Solar System. The nine planets are: Mercury, Venus, Earth, Mars, Jupiter, Saturn, Uranus, Neptune, and Pluto.

The head of the Solar System

The Sun is a huge ball of hot gas. It is 150 million kilometres away from the Earth. Sun is an ordinary star, like the thousands of others you see in the night sky. Without it life is not possible on Earth. People on the Earth have always recognized the importance of the Sun and have often worshiped it as God.

Sun is a hot ball of fire.

Brightness of the Sun

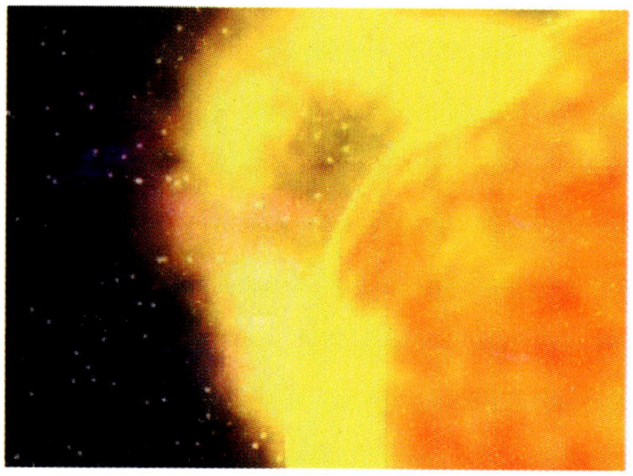

The Sun is the star closest to us.

To many astronomers who study quasars, pulsars, white dwarfs, red giants, black holes and other exotic members of the Universe, the Sun is a fairly dull, average sort of star.

Sun viewed through different filters.

It is but one of one hundred thousand million stars in the Milky Way galaxy, which is but one of the billions of galaxies in the Universe. It appears very bright to us only because it is by far our closest star, the next closest is Alpha Centauri which is more than 250,000 times further away.

Some interesting facts about the Sun

- The Sun is a 'yellow dwarf', a sphere of luminous gas 1,392,000 kilometres in diameter. Its mass is 1.99 x 10^{30} kilograms (1.99 x 10^{27} tonnes), 330,000 times bigger than the Earth.
- The temperature at the core is about 15,000,000 degrees Celsius, but at the surface (the photosphere) it is only about 5,700 degrees Celsius.
- The Sun has an atmosphere - the inner layer, the chromosphere, gives the Sun its colour, and the outer layer, the corona, is much hotter than the photosphere.

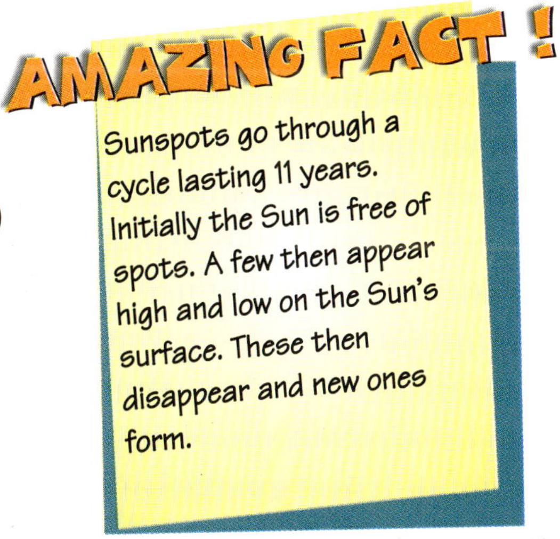

Mercury

Mercury is the first planet from the Sun. It is a small and rocky planet. It is not much larger than the Moon and is the smallest planet after Pluto. The surface of Mercury is pitted with thousands of craters left after meteors crashed into the planet.

Mercury

Mercury

Mercury is the innermost planet of the solar system. It is an airless, lunar-like body. Mercury has been visited by one spacecraft, Mariner-10 in 1974. Its camera shows an atmosphere-less cratered world rather like the Moon. This was expected, though Mercury is hard to study from the Earth; only Pluto is smaller, and Mercury's weak gravity could not hold on to any gases to form an atmosphere.

Mercury and our Moon

The surface of Mercury has thousands of craters on it, just like our Moon. But there are two main differences between the surfaces of the two heavenly bodies. Mercury has no dark, dusty plains and the surface is wrinkled, as though the under-layers have shrunk, leaving the outer skin slightly too large. A huge body must have crashed into Mercury several thousand million year ago, causing a circular area about 1,300 km across which is known as the Caloris Basin.

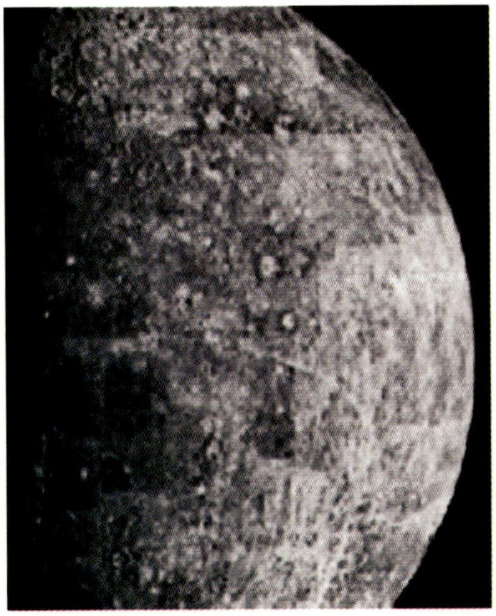

There are craters on Mercury just like our Moon

Characteristics of Mercury

* Mass	: 3.30×10^{26} g
* Radius	: 2,439 km
* Mean density	: 5.4 g / cm^3
* Rotational period	: 58.65 days
* Orbital period	: 88 days
* Mean distance from the Sun	: 57.9 million km

AMAZING FACT !

The Sun beats down furiously on Mercury as it slowly rotates, taking over two months to pass from sunrise to sunset.

Orbit of the planet

Most of the planets have orbits that are almost circular, but Mercury's is an obvious ellipse. Its distance from the Sun changes from 70 million km when farthest away to only 46 km million when nearest, so that from Mercury the Sun sometimes appears one and a half times as large as at other times.

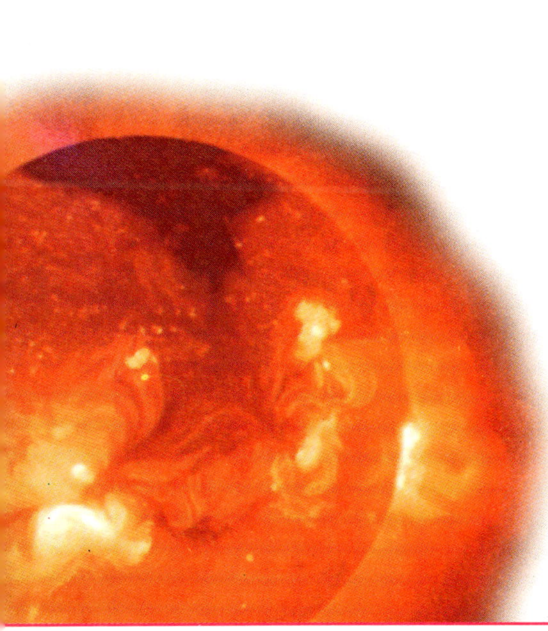

Mercury is the nearest planet to the Sun

Venus

Venus is the second planet from the Sun. It attains the greatest brilliancy in the night sky, outshining all the stars, hence its poetic names 'morning/ evening star'. There are no natural satellites of this planet.

Venus

Venus is the planet that orbits the Sun between the Earth and Mercury, and is almost exactly the same size as the Earth. But it is very different from our planet. The surface of Venus is the hottest place in the Solar System, with a temperature reaching 480°C.

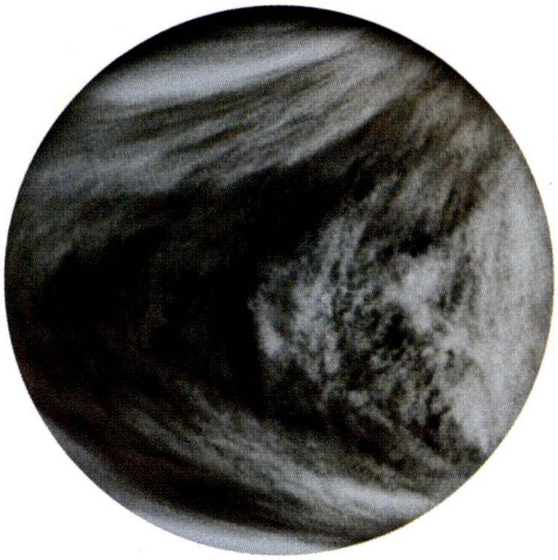
Venus

It is a rocky wind-swept planet with an 'atmosphere' that would feel thicker than ocean water at a depth of several hundred metres.

AMAZING FACT !

The space probe Magellan has sent back to Earth the best pictures yet of Venus till date. The planet is possibly the most unpleasant place in the Solar System.

Venus is the second planet from the Sun

This atmosphere contains carbon dioxide, sulphuric acid and other poisonous compounds, and lightning flickers between the clouds.

Characteristics of Venus

* Mass	: 4.87×10^{24} kg
* Radius	: 6,051 km
* Mean density	: 5.2 g / cm^3
* Equatorial gravity	: 860 cm / s^2
* Rotational period	: 243 days (retrograde)
* Orbital period	: 224.7 days
* Mean distance from the Sun	: 108.2 million km

Greenhouse effect

The Sun's rays fall on the planet's rocky surface that warms up and gives out heat radiation. The carbon dioxide surrounding Venus lets in enough sunlight to heat the surface but does not let out the heat radiated out from the surface. The heat gets trapped, releasing more carbon dioxide from the rocks and making the heat blanket even more effective. This greenhouse effect has turned Venus into an oven.

Greenhouse effect on Venus

Earth

Earth is the third planet from the Sun. It is the planet on which we live. It is a huge rocky ball whose surface is covered with two-thirds of water and one third of land. It is surrounded by layers of air known as atmosphere.

Earth

Earth is one of the nine planets of the solar system. The planet on which we live is not completely round. In fact, it bulges a little at the equator and is rather flattened at the poles, a shape known as an oblate spheroid.

Earth is our home planet.

Origin of the Earth

Earth was formed around 4,600 million years ago, when it was thought to have been a ball of molten rock. The surface was probably as hot as 4000° C. It took many millions of years for the surface to cool down enough for a solid crust to form.

A cloud of gas and dust began to condense under the attraction of gravitational forces to form a solid surface. After millions of years the rock crust and the oceans and atmosphere formed. There was a single land mass about two hundred million years ago. Later it split into smaller land masses, which after millions of years of drift, finally formed the continents present today.

Characteristics of Earth

* Mass	:	5.97×10^{24} kg
* Radius (equatorial)	:	6,378 km
* Mean density	:	5.52 g / cm^3
* Rotational period	:	23 h 56 min 4 s.
* Orbital period	:	365.26 days
* Mean distance from the Sun	:	149.6 million km
* Equatorial gravity	:	978 cm / s^2

AMAZING FACT !

The Earth is constantly moving. It spins round in space like a top, and at the same time it travels around the Sun in an orbit that takes one year to complete.

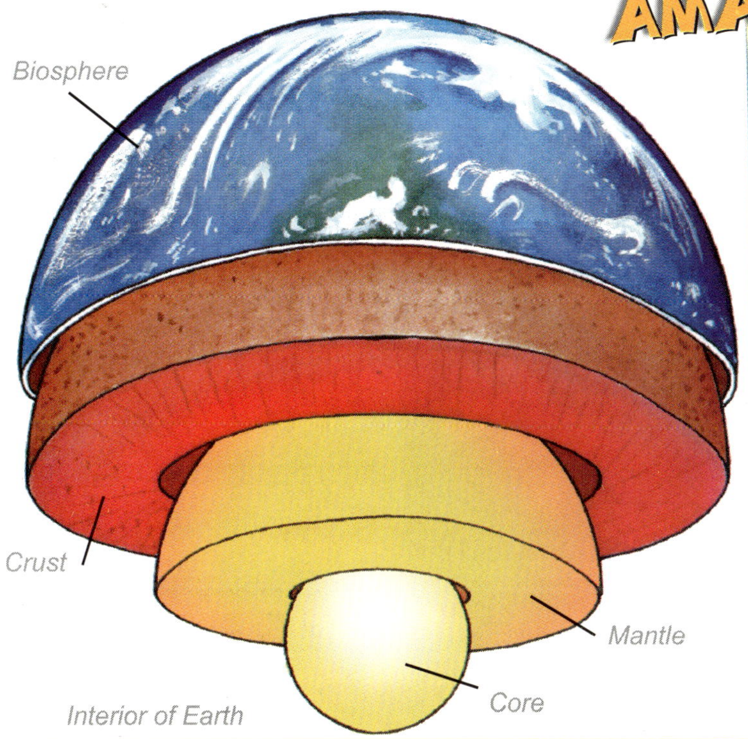

Interior of Earth

The Interior of the planet

The interior of the Earth is differentiated into zones. An iron / nickel-rich molten core which is 3,500 km in radius. An iron- magnesium silicate mantle which is 85% by volume of the Earth, and a crust of lighter metal silicates. The boundary between core and mantle is called the Gutenberg discontinuity; that between mantle and crust is the Mohorovicic (Or Moho) discontinuity.

Moon

Moon is the Earth's only natural satellite, about a quarter the size of the Earth, and lacking any atmosphere. It is treated as one of the family of terrestrial planets.

Moon

The Moon is the natural satellite of the Earth. It revolves round the Earth while the Earth revolves round the Sun. The Moon is made of rock and looks like a small planet. It is just over a quarter of the Earth's size.

Moon

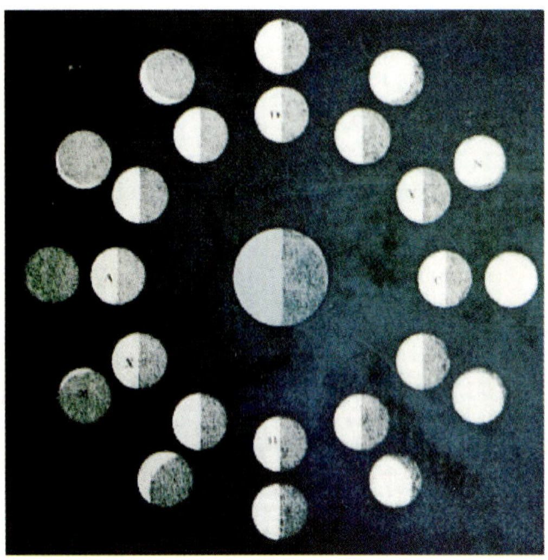

Phases of Moon

Phases of the Moon

It takes the Moon about one month to orbit the Earth. In that time its shape as seen from Earth changes from a thin crescent to a Full Moon and back again. Half of it is lit by the Sun, and the other half is in darkness.

Craters on the surface of Moon

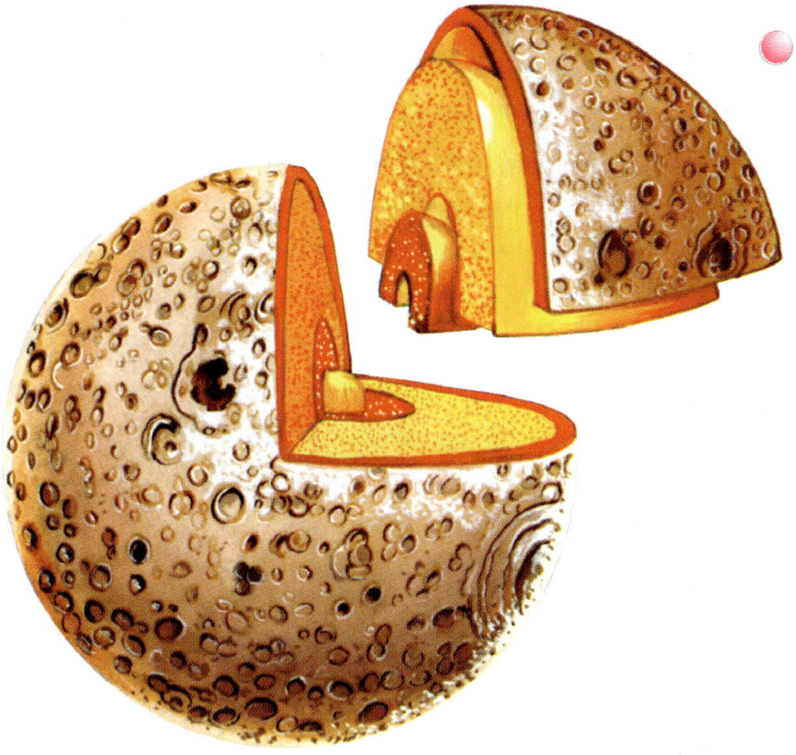

Structure of Moon

Until recently the Moon was thought to have no air or water. But in 1998 the space probe Lunar Prospector found ice at the poles.

At new Moon, the Moon cannot be seen because the dark side is facing the Earth.

As the Moon moves on round the Earth, we see more and more of its sunlit part till we see its fully lit face on full Moon.

Nearly everywhere on the Moon there are craters. Most of them were made by meteorites that crashed onto the Moon.

The Moon does not give out any light of its own.

Characteristics of Moon

* Mass	:	0.073×10^{27} g
* Radius (equatorial)	:	1,738 km
* Mean density	:	3.34 g / cm^3
* Equatorial gravity	:	162 cm / s^2
* Rotational period	:	27.3 days
* Orbital period	:	27.3 days
* Average distance from Earth	:	3,84,400 km

Mars

Mars is the fourth planet from the Sun; the outermost of the terrestrial-type planets, with an eccentric orbit at a mean distance of 228 million km, and a diameter about half that of Earth. Its orbit lies between those the Earth and Jupiter.

Mars

Mars

Mars is the planet nearest to the Earth. It is much smaller and far colder and its atmosphere is very thin. Its mountains and valleys are higher and deeper than anything on the Earth, evidence of violent surface upheavals when it was younger. The surface of Mars is covered with craters, gorges and volcanoes. The volcano Olympus Mons and the canyon named Valles Marineris are the largest volcano and canyon in the Solar System.

Phobos and Deimos

Deimos

Phobos and Deimos are the two small moons of Mars. Phobos is larger than Deimos that measures only 27 km in diameter.

Phobos

It orbits only 6,000 km above the surface of Mars, and its month is of seven hours 39 minutes long. It is slowly spiraling inwards and in around forty million years it will crash into the planet.

Characteristics of Mars

Mass	:	6.24×10^{23} kg
Radius (equatorial)	:	3,393 km
Mean density	:	3.93 g / cm^3
Equatorial gravity	:	372 cm / s^2
Rotational period	:	24 h 37 min 22 s
Orbital period	:	687 days
Mean distance from the Sun	:	228 million km

AMAZING FACT !

An Itallian astronomer, Giovanni Schiaparelli believed that there are narrow lines on Mars. He named them 'channels', meaning rivers or river bed.

Hubble's look at Mars

Hubble Space Telescope pictures of Mars, taken on June 27 in preparation for the July 4 landing of the Pathfinder spacecraft, show a dust storm churning through the deep canyons of Valles Marineris, just 1,000 km south of the Pathfinder spacecraft's landing site.

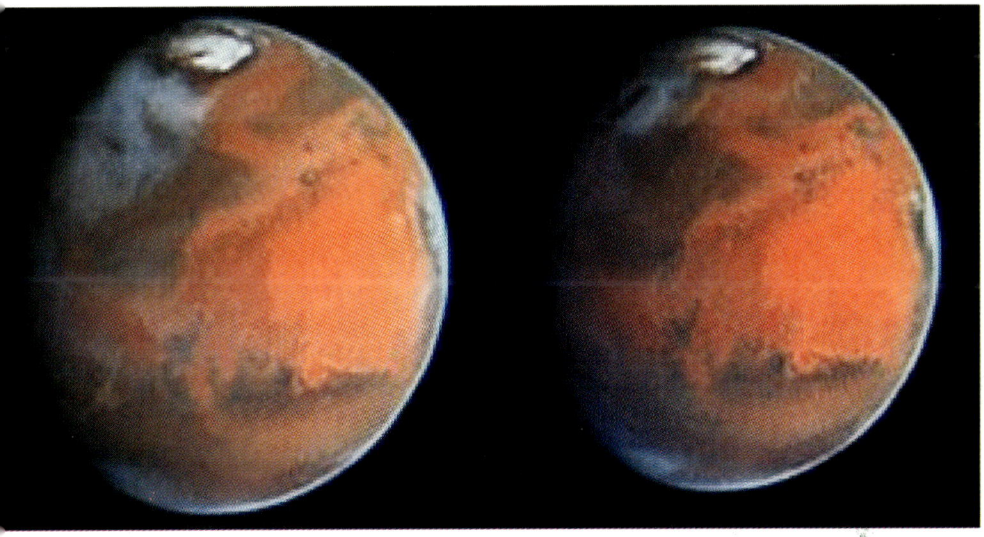

June 27, 1997 July 9, 1997

Asteroids

An asteroid is a tiny planet that revolves around the Sun. Most of them can be found in the wide gap between the orbits of Mars and Jupiter. Some asteroids have unusual orbits.

Asteroids

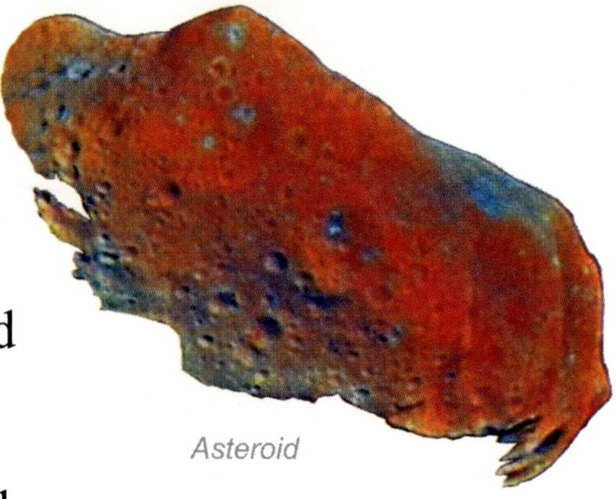

Asteroid

Asteroids are the debris of planets that orbit the Sun. These are the different sized chunks of rock, ranging from specks of dust to some which are a few hundred kilometres across. Asteroids follow different orbits. In the eighteenth century, astronomers were convinced that a missing world existed between Mars and Jupiter. A search was mounted and the first asteroid, Ceres was discovered in 1801.

Known asteroids

Today a large number of asteroids are known. Around two thousand of them have well-determined orbits and revolve around the Sun as part of the 'main belt', in the gap between Mars and Jupiter.
They are tiny, only a handful having a diameter of more than a few tens of kilometres, and the combined mass of all the asteroids is thought to be only a fraction of that of the Moon.

Most asteroids are irregular in shape

Asteroids orbit the Sun, between Mars and Jupiter. The belt that these asteroids form between the planets is known as asteroid belt.

Origin of asteroids

Asteroids are believed to have originated during the formation of the Solar System, when planetesimals accreted from solar nebula. The more primitive carbonaceous asteroids may have evolved little since then, while the other types may have been parts of larger bodies that first accreted and later broke up by collisions.

AMAZING FACT !

The closest recorded encounter happened on 22 March 1989, when a tiny asteroid named 1989, FC passed at less than twice the distance of the Moon.

Recently a few small asteroids have been discovered in highly elliptical orbits that come inside the orbit of Mars, some crossing the orbit of Earth - the Apollo, Amor, and Aten families.

An Asteroid

Jupiter

Jupiter is the fifth planet from the Sun, and the innermost of the giant outer planets. It contains two-thirds of the matter in the Solar System, apart from the Sun. In recent years it has been observed in close-up by Pioneer 10 and 11 spacecrafts and by Voyagers 1 and 2.

Jupiter

Jupiter is the largest planet in the solar system. It is so large that a thousand Earths could fit inside it. But it spins so fast that its day is less than 10 hours long. This rapid spin has made its equator bulge outwards.

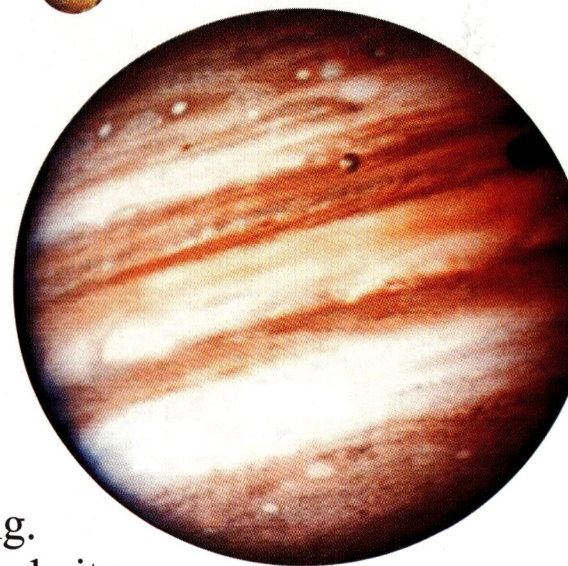

Jupiter

Family portrait of Jupiter's large moons

Moons of Jupiter

The Jovian moons number more than 60, including the four large satellites namely Callisto, Europa, Io, Ganymede discovered by Galileo, which are distinct worlds in themselves and lie in near-circular orbits in an equatorial plane.

Characteristics of Jupiter

Mass	:	$1{\cdot}901 \times 10^{27}$ kg
Equatorial radius	:	71,400 km
Polar radius	:	66,750 km
Mean density	:	$1{\cdot}33$ g / cm^3
Rotational period	:	9 h 55 min 41 s
Orbital period	:	11·9 years
Mean distance from the Sun	:	778.34 million km

AMAZING FACT !

Jupiter has a diameter of 142,200 km at the poles and has mass 318 times that of Earth.

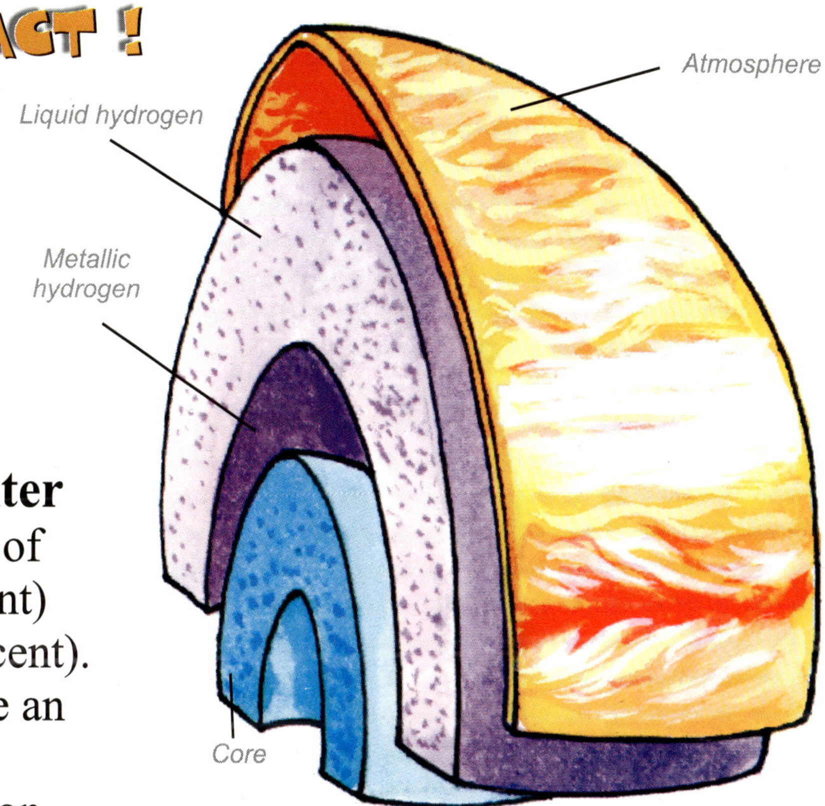

Structure of Jupiter

Structure of Jupiter

It is primarily made of hydrogen (82 per cent) and helium (17 per cent). It is believed to have an innermost core of terrestrial composition of 5-10. Earth masses, a large outer core of hydrogen and helium in a metallic phase, a liquid hydrogen/ helium mantle, and a deep gaseous atmosphere. The planet has a significant internal source of heat, and radiates twice as much heat from inside as it receives from the Sun.

Saturn

Saturn is the sixth planet from the Sun, notable for its ring system - first seen by Galileo in 1610, and first explained by Huygens in 1656. It has 33 known moons, the largest of which, Titan, has an atmosphere.

Saturn

Saturn used to be known as the planet with 'the rings'. Ring systems have now been discovered around its three neighbouring planets but Saturn's rings are by far the brightest. This planet rotates very fast but not faster than Jupiter and this rapid rotation causes it to bulge at its equator and flatten at its poles.

Saturn

Rings of Saturn

The rings of Saturn were observed in close-up by Voyager spacecraft. The rings have particle-size distribution ranging up to several metres. They are probably made of water and ice possibly created by break-up of a moon which came too near Saturn. The rings show a complex structure including several divisions and innumerable 'ringlets'.

Rings of Saturn

Characteristics of Saturn

* Mass	:	5.69×10^{26} kg
* Equatorial radius	:	60,000 km
* Polar radius	:	53,500 km
* Mean density	:	$0.69\ g / cm^3$
* Rotational period	:	10 h 14 m
* Orbital period	:	29.5 years
* Inclination of equator	:	27°
* Mean distance from the Sun	:	1,427 million km.

AMAZING FACT !

Two of Saturn's moons are Titan and Mimas. Titan is the largest and is the only moon in the solar system with an atmosphere. Mimas orbits closest to the planet.

Moons of Saturn

Structure of Saturn

Like Jupiter, Saturn is also a hydrogen / helium planet with a presumed innermost core of rocky composition and several Earth masses.

An outer core of metallic hydrogen and helium, a liquid mantle of hydrogen / helium, and an atmosphere about 1,000 km deep.

It is also believed to have several cloud layers, solid ammonia, ammonium hydro sulphide, water ice, and water-ammonia.

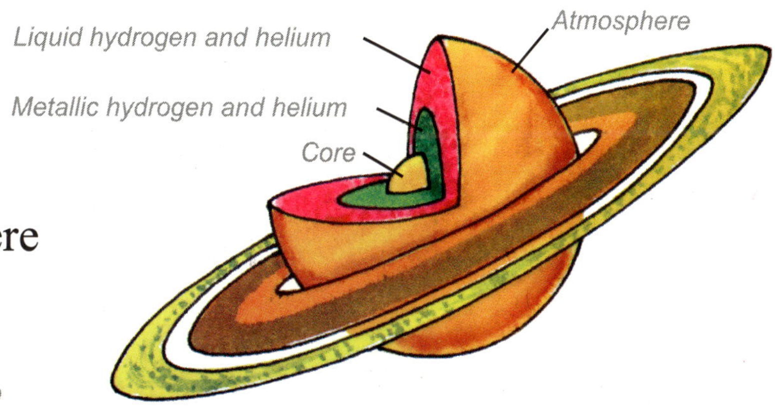

Structure of Saturn

Uranus

Uranus is the seventh planet from the Sun. Discovered by W Herschel in 1781, it is a smaller 'gas giant' than Jupiter or Saturn, and a near-twin of Neptune. It is accompanied by at least 27 moons and a faint ring system.

Uranus

Uranus

Uranus is surrounded by a thick atmosphere of helium, hydrogen and methane. But unlike the other 'cloudy' planets, it has hardly any cloud markings.
The most exciting thing about Uranus is the tilt of its axis. The axis is so tipped over that during its 'year' the Sun can shine almost overhead at each pole, and parts of its surface are bathed in continuous day, and night, for almost 40 years of the Earth.

Satellites of Uranus

For many years five satellites of Uranus had been known. Out of them Titania is the largest, having the diameter of 1,600 km. The smallest Miranda is around 480 km across. All satellites are airless, icy-surfaced bodies with craters where flying fragments crashed into them. Voyager has discovered 10 new satellites of the planet which are less than 50 km across; 12 more were discovered later.

Miranda, a moon of Uranus

Characteristics of Uranus

* Mass	:	8.7×10^{25} kg
* Radius	:	25,500 km
* Mean density	:	1.3 g / cm^3
* Rotational period	:	17.2 h
* Orbital period	:	84.01 years
* Inclination of equator	:	82°
* Mean distance from the Sun	:	2.87 billion km

A faint ring around Uranus

AMAZING FACT !

Uranus has a faint ring system around it. Voyager 2 sent back close-up observations in 1986, although the ring system was discovered in 1977.

Structure of Uranus

Uranus is mainly composed of hydrogen and helium, just like Jupiter and Saturn. Uranus has a larger percentage of ammonia and methane. Its interior lacks sharp compositional boundaries, but has a rock-rich core, ice-rich mantle, and deep atmosphere. Its low temperature allows condensation of methane clouds, with ammonia and water clouds also likely at lower levels.

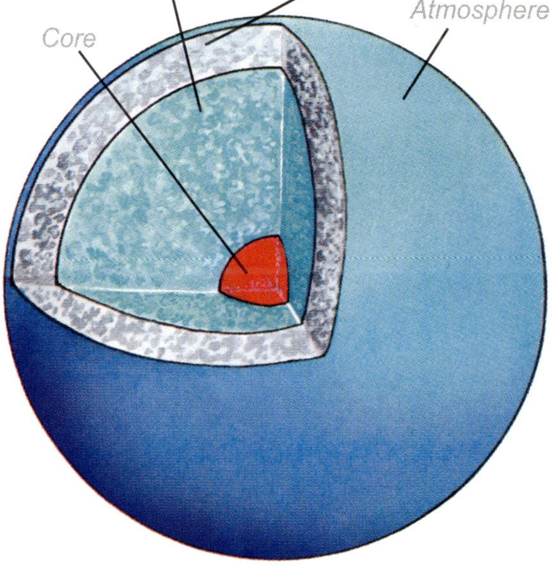

Structure of Uranus

Neptune

Neptune is the eighth planet from the Sun. It is made-up mainly of liquid and frozen gases. Much of our knowledge of Neptune comes from the space probe Voyager, which passed Neptune in the year 1989.

Neptune

Neptune

Neptune is an apparent twin of Uranus internally, composed of hydrogen and helium, but with much more carbon, nitrogen and oxygen than Jupiter and Saturn.

The outermost of the four 'gas giant' planets, discovered in the year 1846 as a result of a prediction by the French astronomer Urbain Leverrier. There are at least 13 moons, including Triton, which has a thin atmosphere, and Nereid.

The blue colour of Neptune

Neptune is thought to lack sharp internal boundaries between a rock-rich core, an ice-rich mantle, and a deep atmosphere. Its bluish-green colour is due to methane in the upper atmosphere. It has cirrus clouds of methane above high-level clouds of methane and ammonia, with lower water clouds.

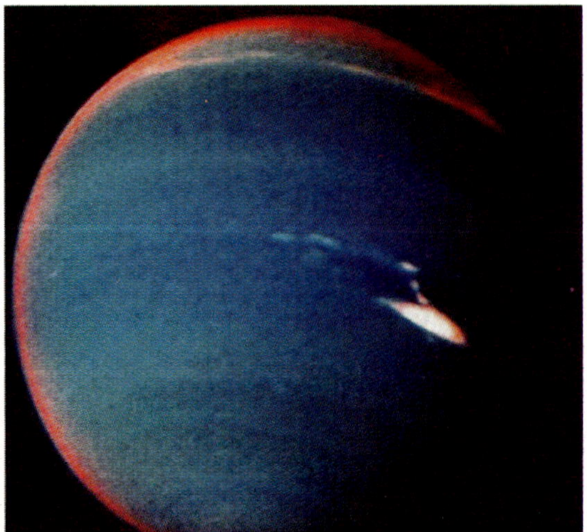

The blue colour of Neptune is due to the presence of methane

Characteristics of Neptune

* Mass	:	102.7×10^{24} kg
* Radius	:	24,750 km
* Mean density	:	1.7 g / cm^3
* Rotational period	:	0.67 days
* Inclination of equator	:	29.6°
* Orbital period	:	164.8 years
* Mean distance from the Sun	:	4,497 million km

AMAZING FACT !

Triton is Neptune's largest moon, 2,700 km in diameter and covered in icy mountains. It orbits the planet in the opposite direction to the other moons.

Triton, the largest Moon of Neptune

Neptune was discovered by German astronomers in 1846

Discovery of Neptune

John Couch Adams was a British astronomer who in 1844, by studying the motion of Uranus, worked out the position of Neptune before it was discovered, as did the French scientist Urbain Leverrier in 1846. The planet was actually discovered in that year by German astronomers J. Galle and H. D'Arrest.

Pluto

Pluto is the ninth and most distant planet from the Sun. Smaller than our Moon, it was discovered in 1930 by Clyde Tombaugh after an extensive search. It is an anomalous planet in the outer Solar System, bearing no resemblance to the 'gas giants'.

Pluto

Pluto

Pluto is named after the Greek God of the underworld. Pluto is the only planet in the solar system which has not been visited by a spacecraft. The orbit of Pluto is the most elliptical of all the planets and in 1989 it was at its 'perihelion', when it came closer to the Sun than Neptune. Pluto is so small that it is only about one-sixth of the diameter of the Earth.

Discovery of Pluto

Much effort was devoted at Lowell Observatory in USA, to the search for Planet X, and the search was continued after the death of astronomer Percival Lowell in 1916. Eventually, in 1930, the planet now known as Pluto was discovered there by Clyde William Tombaugh, though it is now clear that Lowell's prediction had no scientific validity and that it was only by chance that it was discovered.

Clyde Tombaugh

Characteristics of Pluto

* Mass	:	11.94×10^{21} kg
* Radius	:	1,150 km
* Mean density	:	2.0 g / cm^3
* Rotational period	:	6.387 days
* Inclination of equator	:	120°
* Orbital period	:	248.5 years
* Mean distance from the Sun	:	5,900 million km

AMAZING FACT !

Charon is named after the ferryman who took people across the river Styx, which was the only way into the underworld.

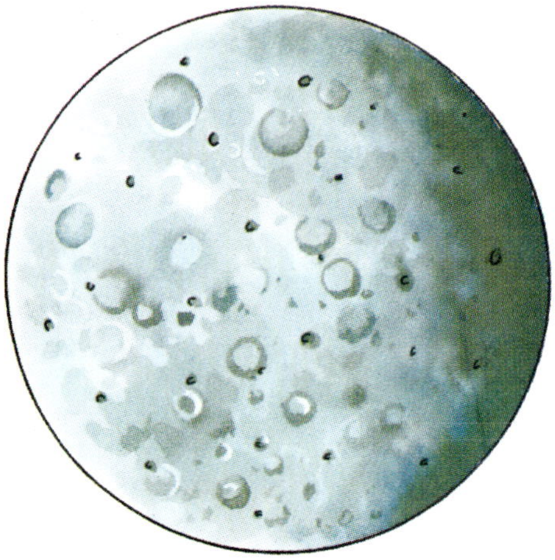

Charon, satellite of Pluto

Moon of Pluto

Pluto's only known satellite, Charon was discovered photographically in the year 1978. Its distance from Pluto is around 19.1 million km and its diameter is around 1,200 km.

It is unusually huge, relative to its planet, and has a surface of mainly water ice.

Pluto's satellite is approximately 1/3rd the size of Pluto

Comets

A comet is a member of the solar system, orbiting the Sun. The solid part of a comet, the nucleus, is very small (a few kilometres across) but the cloud of gas and dust boiling away from the nucleus, the tail, can stretch out millions of kilometres.

Comets

Comets are icy objects which travel through the solar system. A bright comet in the night sky looks like a hazy patch with a long wispy tail. Comets travel in orbits through the solar system. They evaporate gas and dust and grow long tails when they are near enough to the Sun's heat and light.

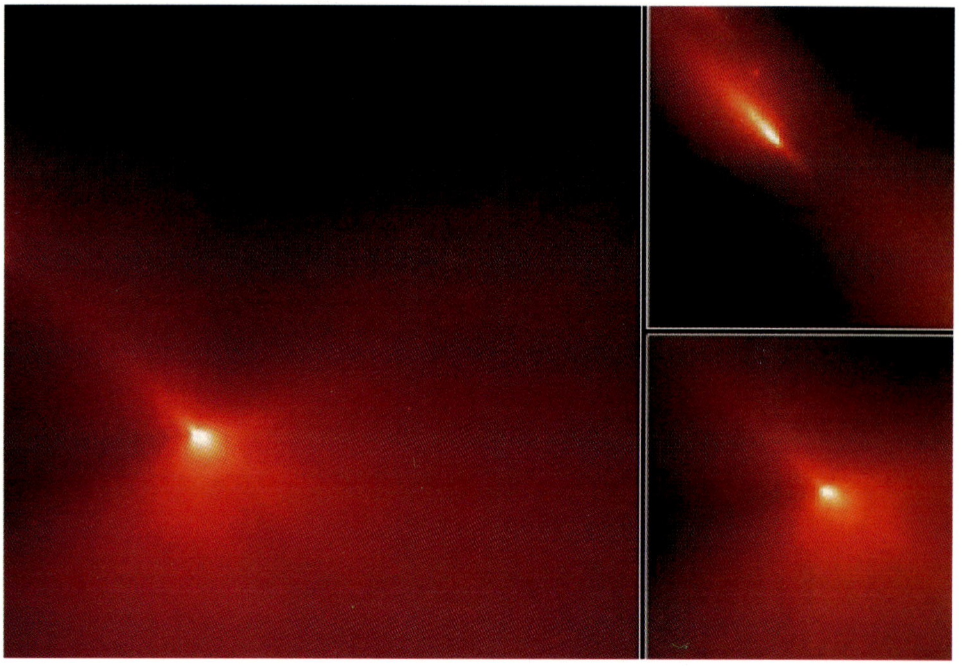

Comet Hyakutake as taken with the Hubble telescope

The tails always point away from the Sun, blown by the light and streams of atomic particles from the Sun. The most famous comet, Halley's Comet, can be seen from the Earth every 76 years.

AMAZING FACT !

Comets that are bright enough to be seen easily by the naked eye are quite rare, but astronomers using telescopes find 20 or 30 comets every year.

Halley's Comet

Halley's comet

Halley's comet is the most famous of all comets, recorded by Chinese astronomers in 467 BC (and possibly in 611 BC). It is a periodic comet orbiting the Sun in a retrograde direction with a period of 76 years. It is named after the English astronomer Edmund Halley, who applied to comets Newton's theory of planetary motions and correctly predicted the return of the bright comet in the year 1758.

Orbits of comets

Every comet has a tail at its end

Comets are believed to be left over particles from beginning of the Solar System, when most of these particles collided with each other to build up the planets. The comet nuclei, containing crumbly rock particles trapped in frozen ice, were left. If their orbits take them near the Sun, the heat turns the outer ice to vapour and the solid particles are released as dust. In their frozen state far from the Sun, comets are invisible. Each time a comet passes near the Sun it pours some more of its nucleus into space. Eventually it 'dies' and becomes just an orbiting rock.

Comet's nucleus

Meteors and Meteorites

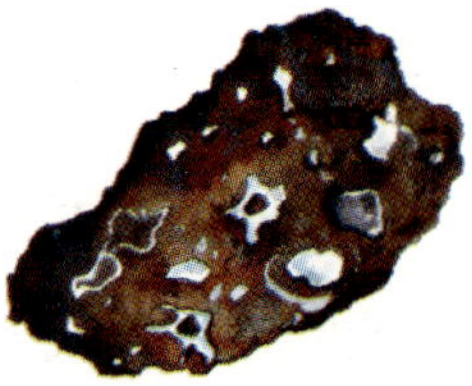

A meteor is a particle sometimes as small as a sand grain hurtling at up to 40 km into the atmosphere. Meteorites are bodies from space that are large enough to reach the ground without burning up in the atmosphere as meteors do.

Meteors

Meteors are the hot glowing pieces of rocks and dust from space that plunge into the Earth's atmosphere.

Meteor crater

Most meteors burn up above an altitude of 100 km. If you gaze at the stars for half an hour on a clear night, you will see an occasional streak of light, which is a meteor's glowing trail.

Shooting Stars

The common name for meteors is 'shooting stars'. But they are not really stars. As the particles of dust and pieces of rocks enter the Earth's atmosphere, most of them burn up completely. When they do this, we just see the red-hot flash that we call a meteor. As the Earth travels round the Sun, it sometimes passes through swarms of meteors. On these days we can see showers of meteors all of which seem to come from a small area of the sky.

Meteorite

Meteorites

Shower of meteors

Meteorites are pieces of rocks from space which are big enough to fall to the ground. About 500 large ones strike the Earth each year. There are three main kinds of meteorites: some are stony, some are nearly all iron, and some are a mixture. They are different from the rocks the Earth is made of, so scientists like to find and study them.

AMAZING FACT !

Some meteorites are mostly metals (iron and nickel), while others are made of stone. These may be fragments from asteroids that later broke up in collision.

Reaching the Earth

A falling meteorite will leave a brilliant trail in the sky known as a fire ball, but very few meteorites have been found by tracking fire balls. Since they can look like ordinary dark stones, most meteorites have been discovered by special searches in area where they stand out, such as the snow fields of Antarctica.

Astronomy

Astronomy is the oldest science of studying Sun, Moon and other heavenly bodies. Astronomers survey this huge volume of space, where there are many different things to study. It is just because of astronomy that we know so much about the spaces beyond.

Astronomy

The word 'astronomy' comes from the Greek words **astron** meaning 'star' and **nomia** meaning 'arrangement'. Astronomy is the study of the planets, stars and galaxies that make up the Universe. Astronomers try to explain all the things that you can see in the night sky.

Interstellar gas and dust in the Eagle Nebula

History of Astronomy

Early astronomers watched the movements of the Sun, Moon and the stars in order to keep track of time and the seasons. From late antiquity to the seventeenth century, astronomy had two related goals: to show that the movements of the planets were not haphazard but regular and therefore predictable, and to predict them with accuracy. All else that concerned astronomers was peripheral.

In early times, astronomer used to predict movements in the Universe with the help of various signs and symbols.

Modern Astronomy

Modern astronomers make observations with the help of telescopes usually in large observatories. Telescopes gather the light from objects that are too faint to see with the naked eye. As well as sending out light, stars and galaxies also give out other kinds of radiations like, x-rays and radio waves. Astronomers detect these rays with the help of sophisticated telescopes, space satellites and other equipments.

An astronomical observatory

AMAZING FACT !

The Hubble Space Telescope can send us pictures of distant objects because it is above the Earth's atmosphere.

Milestone in Astronomy

270 BC	Aristarchus teaches that the Earth orbits the Sun.
1608	Lippershey invents the telescope.
1600s	Kepler proposes that the planets' orbits are ellipses.
1687	Newton publishes theory of gravity.
1920	Distant galaxies are discovered to be flying away at great speeds.
1929	Hubble demonstrates that the Universe is expanding.
1963	Background radiation, thought to be from the Big Bang, is discovered.
1992	Ripples in background radiation confirm Big Bang theory.

Space Exploration

Space exploration has provided details about Neptune, in-depth exploration of Mars and Venus, and detailed study of the Moon. The study of comets and asteroids is less advanced. Humans have landed on the Moon. They have stayed long on space station. But space exploration still remains dangerous and costly.

Space exploration

Since the beginning of the Space Age in 1957, human beings have continuously looked for new ways of exploring space. Astronauts have walked on the Moon's surface, and can now live and work for months in space stations. The Space Age began in October 1957, when the Soviet Union launched the artificial satellite Sputnik 1 into orbit around the Earth.

AMAZING FACT !

The three - stage, 110 metre Saturn 5 rocket lifted American astronauts on way to the Moon. Of this, only the Command Module returned to Earth.

The astronauts go in the space by rockets or spacecrafts.

Journey to the Moon

The exploration of the Moon began even before the first person had flown in space, when the unmanned Soviet spacecraft Luna 1 flew past the Moon in January 1959. In 1966 the probe Luna 9 made the first soft landing on its surface. In July 1969 three US astronauts flew to the Moon in the Apollo 11 spacecraft. The main spacecraft, piloted by astronaut Michael Collins, orbited the Moon, while Neil Armstrong and Edwin Aldrin landed in the tiny Lunar Module. During five more Moon missions, the last in 1972, astronauts explored the Moon's surface, collecting rock samples and setting up scientific equipment. More recently, in 1994, the probe Clementine spent two months orbiting the Moon and mapping its surface.

An astronaut exploring the Moon

Unit – 3

About Earth

Structure of Earth

The Earth is one of the nine planets in the solar system. It is a huge rocky ball whose surface is two thirds water and one third land. The Earth comprises three layers : crust, mantle and core.

Three layers of Earth

When you peel an orange, you only remove a thin outer covering. In the similar way the surface of the Earth is only a thin layer compared to what lies beneath.

Earth

People conceived of this imaginary fearsome edge of the flat earth.

AMAZING FACT !

Until about 500 years ago, people thought that the Earth was flat and feared that if they sailed too far in one direction, they would topple over the edge.

The Earth is made-up of three layers : crust, mantle and core. Crust is the thin layer of rocks. Heat from inside the Earth makes some of the rocks in mantle to melt, while the great pressure inside the layers below, compresses the rock into a solid state. Core is the centre of the Earth which has a liquid metal outer layer and a solid metal interior.

Crust

Crust is just a thin layer of rocks that covers the surface of Earth. Life exists on this layer itself. This layer is made-up of hard rocks and is covered with water at many places. The crust is about 5 km thick under the oceans and up to 30 km thick under the land.

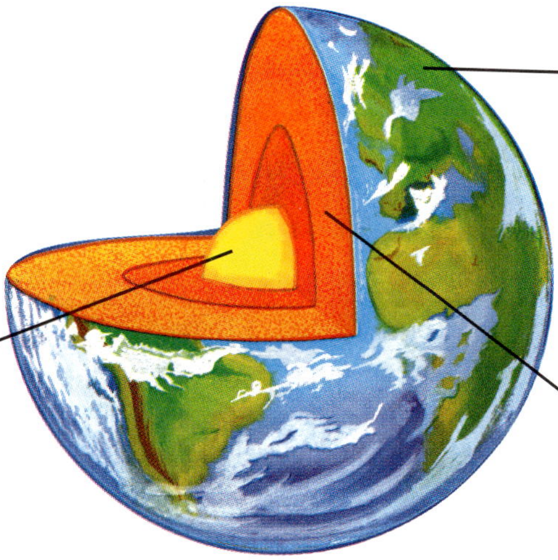

There are three layers of Earth : crust, mantle and core.

Core

Core, the centre of the Earth, is a dense ball of hot rocks and metals. Core can further be divided into two parts : outer core and inner core. Outer core is made-up mainly of nickel and iron but with a certain amount of lighter materials such as silicon and sulphur. This layer surrounds the solid in a core that is made-up of an iron-nickel alloy under pressure.

Mantle

Mantle is the layer that lies just below the crust. This layer is made-up of molten rocks. Within the mantle the material rises and falls as a result of heating and cooling of the material. These movements are thought to be what makes the continents move.

The Continents

A Continent is any one of the seven main land masses of the world: Europe, Asia, North America, South America, Africa, Australia, and Antarctica. Continents occupy less than one third of the Earth's surface.

Emergence of Continents

About 300 million years ago, all the Continents existed together forming a single vast supercontinent known as Pangaea.

This supercontinent then split into two parts: a northern section called Laurasia and a southern section called Gondwana. The two land masses thus formed gradually broke further into smaller pieces to form the seven Continents that we know today.

AMAZING FACT !

The plates move about at the rate of 2.5 cm, which is about the same rate as our fingernails grow.

The major land masses on the Earth's surface are called Continents. They occupy around one third of the Earth's surface area.

Plate tectonics

The rocky surface of the Earth is divided into several large plates. These plates float on the hot, molten rocks in the mantle beneath. Heat from the Earth's inside makes the plates move, carrying the continents with them. The explanation of these plate movements is known as plate tectonics.
As the plates move, mountains and underwater ridges, deep trenches, and huge valleys form at the edge of the plates.

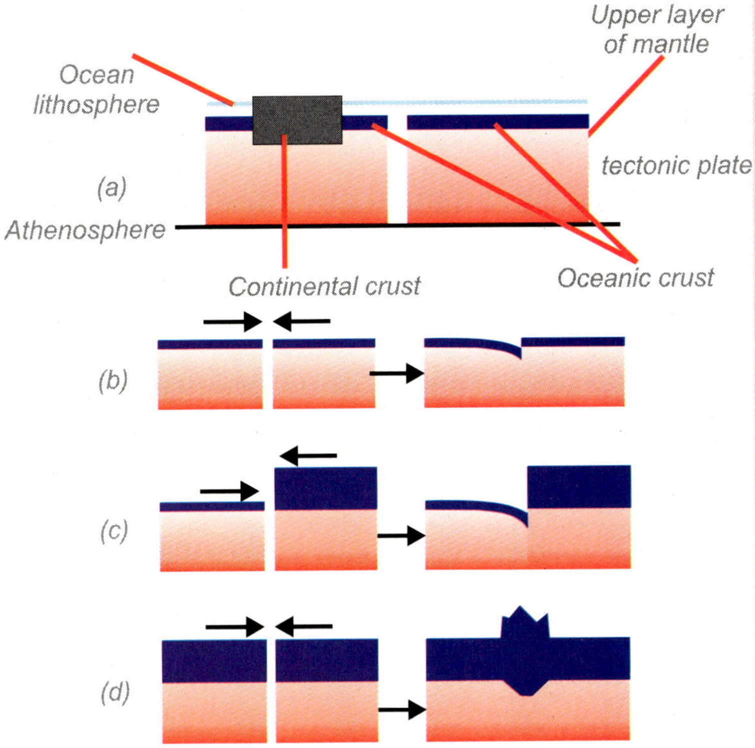

The movements of the plates create mountains, valleys, trenches and ridges.

Continental Drift

Thc cvidence of the fact that the Continents gradually drifted to their present positions is also available. Africa and South America fit neatly together. Identical fossils of ferns and reptiles have been found in Africa, South America, Australia and Antarctica. These animals and plants could not have crossed the oceans, so they must have lived on the same land mass long time back.

Continental drift results from the movement of the crustal plates in relation to one another.

Rocks and Minerals

The land on which we live is made-up of rocks. All the rocks in the world are made up of chemicals called minerals. When seen through a microscope, a rock shows the crystals of different minerals that it is made of. Each mineral has its own chemical composition and there are usually no more than half a dozen in each rock.

What are rocks ?

Rocks are the hard, solid material that make-up the Earth. They can be found in hillsides and mountains, in cliffs along the seashore, in walls of large building, as the broken pieces of stone on the surface of the road.

Such mushroom rocks are formed when huge rocks are attacked by the process of erosion and weathering caused by the action of wind.

Rocks also lie under the oceans and seas and beneath the ice in polar regions. Every kind of rock is made-up of one or more minerals.

Halite

AMAZING FACT !

Table salt comes from the mineral halite. Halite forms where sea water drys at the shore. Pure salt has no colour, but impurities in halite give it pink colour.

Types of rocks

There are three main types of rocks: igneous, sedimentary and metamorphic.
Igneous rocks are formed at high temperatures from molten rocky material, either deep within the Earth or on the surface.
Sedimentary rocks are formed from mud and sand (sediments) that have been deposited on land or in ancient rivers, lakes or seas.
Metamorphic rocks are formed from sedimentary or igneous rocks that have been buried and heated up or put under great pressure.

Sedimentary rock

Igneous rock

Minerals

Minerals are solid crystalline material that form the building materials of rocks. They include everyday substances such as rock salt, asbestos, the graphite in our pencil lead, the talc use to make talcum powder, and the china clay use to make crockery. They also include metals like gold and silver and the ores of metals such as tin, iron and copper.

AMAZING FACT !

The biggest diamond ever found is the Kohinoor.
It has an ultimate shine and is the most expensive diamond.

Metamorphic rock

Diamond

Minerals that are known for their beauty and rarity are called gems. Some rocks comprise just one mineral, while some contain many.Scientists have discovered over 2,500 different minerals, but some of them are very rare.

Graphite

Volcanoes

A volcano is a mountain or hill giving out lava which comes from deep inside the Earth's surface. Whenever a volcano erupts, lava and ash build up to form a cone. Some volcanoes liberate clouds of ash and gas when they erupt. Others have streams of lava flowing down their sides.

Birth of a volcano

Volcanoes are formed when the magma inside the Earth forces its way up through the cracks in the crust and spills out as lava.

When a volcano erupts, broken rocks and ash are thrown out with the lava. The large lumps are defined as volcanic bombs.

As the rock and ash cool, they make layers of solid rock. As magma rises, gases separate out from the molten rock and collect near the surface causing great explosions.

Broken rocks and ash are thrown out in a volcanic eruption

AMAZING FACT !

When Mount Vesuvius in Southern Italy erupted in the year AD 79, the town of Pompeii was completely buried under volcanic ash.

Mount Vesuvius

Where do they take place ?

Volcanic eruptions occur in those parts of the Earth's crust where there is a large flow of heat from inside. This is usually along the margins of plates that carry land and sea.

An erupting volcano produces thousands of tonnes of lava.

Types of volcanoes

Volcanoes are mainly of three types: active, dormant and extinct. Active volcanoes are those which have erupted in the recent past. A volcano that has not erupted for a long time is said to be dormant, although there is always the danger that it may erupt all of a sudden. When people think that a volcano is finally dead, they call it an extinct volcano. This shows that volcanoes eventually die. The volcanoes are slowly eroded.

The softer rocks are eroded first and in some places the only part remaining is the hard plug which once filled the vent of the volcano.

Some volcanoes liberate clouds of ash and gas when they erupt.

Earthquakes

An earthquake is a series of shock waves which result from a break in the rocks deep inside the crust of the Earth. When these waves pass through Earth, they cause further movements. Earthquakes mostly occur at the edges of the plates and may be associated with volcanic activity.

How do they occur ?

Earthquakes take place when the surface of the Earth moves. The Earth's crust consist of several vast plates of solid rocks. These plates move very slowly and sometimes slide past one another. Most severe earthquakes are caused where the plates meet. Sometimes the edges of the plates grasp each other and cannot move, so pressure builds up. Because of this phenomenon, the plate suddenly slip past each other and shake the land violently.

Earthquakes can flatten an entire city in just a few seconds.

Bhuj in Gujarat was totally devastated

The Bhuj earthquake that shook Gujarat on the morning of January 26, 2001 (Republic Day) is one of the two most deadly earthquakes to strike India in its recorded history. One month after the earthquake, government of India figures placed the death toll at 19,727 and the number of injured at 166,000.

Measuring the earthquakes

The intensity of an Earthquake is measured on the Richter Scale, which runs from 0 to 9. This scale measures the forces involved and the effects of the earthquake.

The severity of Earthquake is measured by the richter scale.

Intensity of earthquakes

A small earthquake feels like a distant rumble but the serious one destroys the entire city. The earthquakes focus is usually no more than 100 km. below the surface. The point on the Earth's surface directly above this is the epicenter. Destruction is usually the greatest at this point.

Tsunami Devastation

Early in the morning after Christmas in 2004, the tsunami waves caused immense destruction and devastation mostly in South and South-east Asia. In the aftermath of the tsunami, the scientific verdict has been unanimous– damage is greatest where beaches have been built on, dunes flattened, where ground water was pumped out and coral reefs killed.

The human tragedy in all the these countries and regions has been devastating.

A view of Tsunami a few seconds later

AMAZING FACT !

Earthquakes occuring on the ocean floor produce a wave called tsunami which races towards the shore and destroys buildings carrying boats far inland.

Ice and Glaciers

A glacier is a large body of ice which may form in a mountain valley or in an area, such as the polar regions where the volume of the snow falling in the cold season of the year is greater than the amount which melts during the warmer season.

Formation of Glaciers

You might have noticed that when you squeeze some snow in your hands it holds together. It happens because the pressure of your hands turns the snow particles into ice crystals. The similar things takes place when huge masses of snow build up on top of each other, compressing the layers below.

A body of ice originating from recrystallized snow in mountain valleys and flowing slowly downslope by creep under its own weight makes a glacier.

Snow compressed in a hollow forms a mass of ice that moves slowly down hill towards the lower slopes of the valley. This is defined as a glacier.

AMAZING FACT !

The largest iceberg, seen in the South Pacific Ocean in November 1956, stretched up to 31,000 sq km.

Some Icebergs are really dangerous. One of them sank the unsinkable ship named "Titanic" on which even a movie has been made.

Ice sheets and icebergs

Icebergs are found in large numbers in Antarctica

Ice sheets are the large regions of ice and snow permanently covering the land. The world's greatest ice sheets exist in Antarctica.

Icebergs are huge lumps of ice that break away from ice sheets and glaciers and float on the sea. Only about a ninth of an icebergs appears above the surface. The hidden part under the water is much wider than the visible part.

The largest icebergs break away from the edge of Antarctica, such as from the Ross Ice Shelf. They begin to melt as they drift away from the polar regions. Cold currents carry them great distances.

Ice age

Ice age is the name given to a period of the Earth's history when great ice sheets covered large areas of Earth. Ice ages are also known as glacial epochs. One important result of an ice age is the lowering of the sea level throughout the world as water turns to ice.

In an ice age, the average temperature of the atmosphere falls over a large part of the globe and ice sheets cover large areas of Earth.

Within any ice age there are glacial periods that are cold and interglacial periods that are warmer. The Earth is now passing through the interglacial period. However 10,000 years ago, glacial period existed and the ice spread across wide areas of the Northern Hemisphere.

Oceans 

Pacific Ocean is the world's largest and deepest ocean, extending from the Arctic to Antarctica and from the America to Asia. The average depth of the Pacific is 4,300 m. The ocean floor is made of plateaus, ridges, trenches and sea mountains.

Pacific Islands

There are about 10,000 islands in the Pacific Ocean, spread over a very large area. The islands can be divided into three regions: Micronesia, Melanesia and Polynesia.

Each island region has a distinct group of people with its own way of life. Melanesians are dark-skinned and live in the southwest Pacific. Polynesians are lighter skinned, and live in the eastern Pacific. Micronesians live in the western Pacific.

Most of the islands are coral reefs and volcanic peaks. Coconut palms provide copra (dried coconut flesh) and coconut oil, both important exports.

Underwater landscape

Natural resources and hazards

The ocean is rich in oil and gas fields, fish, marine mammals (seals and whales), sand and gravel aggregates, placer deposits, poly-metallic nodules and precious stones.

Icebergs are common in Davis Strait, Denmark Strait, and the northwestern Atlantic Ocean from February to August and have been spotted as far south as Bermuda and the Madeira Islands; ships subject to superstructure icing in extreme northern Atlantic from October to May; persistent fog can be maritime hazards from May to September.

Life underwater

AMAZING FACT !

Indian Ocean is rich in oil and gas fields, fish, shrimp, sand and gravel aggregates, placer deposits and polymetallic nodules.

Environmental Issues

The endangered marine species include the manatee, seals, sea lions, turtles, and whales; drift net fishing is hastening the decline of fish stocks and contributing to international disputes. Other areas of concern include municipal sludge pollution in eastern US, southern Brazil, and eastern Argentina; oil pollution in Caribbean Sea, Gulf of Mexico, Lake Maracaibo, Mediterranean Sea, and North Sea; industrial waste and municipal sewage pollution in Baltic Sea, North Sea, and Mediterranean Sea.

Waves and Tides

The oceans are always full of energy and liveliness. Local winds push the surface of the oceans into waves which pound onto the shore. The tides wash in and out of harbours twice a day, following the pull of the Sun and the Moon.

Waves in the sea

The wind makes waves in sea by pushing against ripples and making them bigger. The water in a wave does not move from place to place. It moves in a vertical circle, upwards and forwards on the wave crest, then down and back as the wave passes.

Waves are caused by the movement of the wind.

Wave motion

A wave motion is a pattern of disturbance that changes regularly as time passes and the wave moves from one place to another. The waves occurring in the sea are longitudinal waves in which the water molecules move back and forth in the same direction as the direction of the wave.

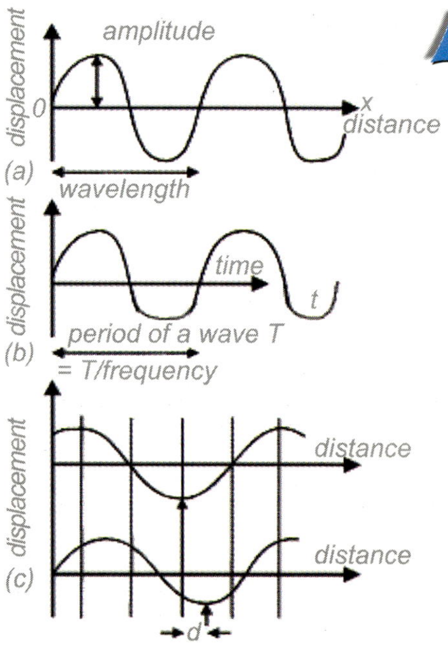

The wave motion changes regularly as time passes.

AMAZING FACT !

High tides send a tidal wave, called a bore, up some rivers. One of the world's highest bores occurs on the Qiantang in China.

What are tides?

Tides are the rise and fall of the sea at regular intervals. At high tide, the sea rises high up the beach. At low tide, it recedes down the beach. The tides are caused by the pull of gravity of the Moon and Sun on the water.

The pull of the Moon makes the water bulge into a high tide on both sides of the Earth. As the Earth spins, each place has a high tide twice a day. The Sun pulls up the water too, but not so strongly. At one time of the month it adds to the Moon's pull. At another, it fights against it.

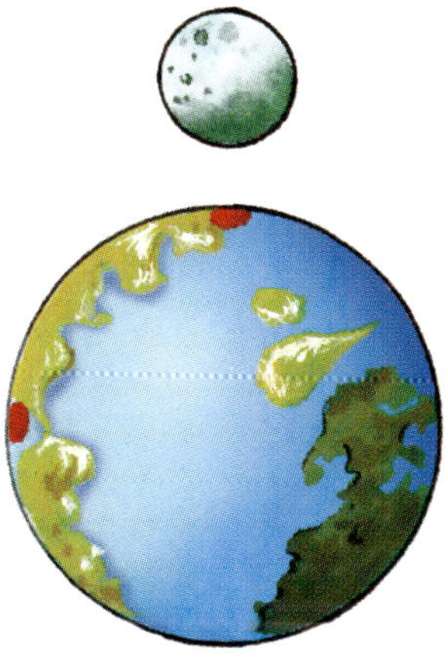

Tides are caused by the pull of the Moon and Sun on the water.

High tide

Low tide

Tidal power

The use of tides as a source of energy to generate electricity is called tidal power. In a tidal power station, a dam is built across the mouth of a river. As the tide comes in and goes out, water rushes in and out of tunnels in the dam. This flow of water turns huge turbines which drive generators.

Life Under Water

Beneath the waves lies another word waiting to be discovered. Sea divers go down to explore the beautiful underwater world. There are fascinating sea creatures and beautifully coloured coral reefs.

Ocean life

It is believed that life began in the oceans millions of years ago. Oceans are home to countless fish, octopuses, seals, sharks and jelly fish. Ocean life is at its richest in the warm shallow waters of coral reefs, where colourful angelfish and butterfly fish live.

Octopus

Shark

Jelly fish

In deeper waters, whales, dolphins and porpoises are found. Most plants live close to the water surface. Apart from these, there exist numerous kinds of microscopic organisms also.

AMAZING FACT !

Most starfish can grow new body parts if the old ones are broken or bitten off. They leave an arm behind to escape a predator.

Seal

Deep sea life

The depths of the sea form the largest habitat of life on Earth. The deep sea creatures are well adapted to survive under high pressure and in absolute darkness. Deep sea fish usually have enormous mouth and long, back curved teeth for grabbing and swallowing anything that swims by.

Crab

Sea Anemones

Shrimps

Shell fish

These fish have huge stomachs which stretch to hold prey that is even bigger than the predator. Some of the commonly found deep sea creatures are anemones, worms, sea cucumbers, brittlestars, crabs, prawns, shellfish, sea squids, shrimps and jellyfish.

Freshwater ecosystems

The waters of tiny pools and great lakes, and the flowing waters of mountain streams and wide rivers are all freshwater ecosystems. Some pools and rivers are non-perennial and appear only in the wet season, so only simple communities live here.

But large rivers and lakes contain complex communities that have developed over hundreds of years.

Rivers and lakes are home to several species of water animals.

Wetlands

Wetlands are damp, boggy areas where water lies on the surface forming lakes and pools, or where plants have grown out into open water to form marshes or swamps. Wetlands support a large variety of plants and animals and their value to humans is enormous.

Importance of Wetlands

Wetlands are rich in food sources. Many small animals exist in the soft ground and provide food for frogs, toads and long-legged birds. Wetlands are also important stopover places for migrating birds.

Wetlands soak up water during storms and let it drain away gradually. Also in some places, wetlands ensure that the water supply for the local cities is good enough to drink.

AMAZING FACT !

Mudskippers, the small fish living in mangrove swamps, can stay out of water for long by breathing mixture of air and water stored in their gill chambers.

Wetlands are marshy areas that soak up water during the rains and ensure good water supply

Types of wetlands

There are many different kinds of wetlands. Some are formed naturally and some because of human activities.

Some wetlands are formed when mud builds up on shores of estuaries. At the mouth of large rivers, this mud forms big deltas. Plants that can survive the salty water conditions form salt marshes here.

The coasts of some tropical seas are fringed with mangrove swamps. These swamps are home to many different creatures.

Vast areas of the cooler parts of the world are covered in peat bogs. These are formed by remarkable plants called bog mosses, which are able to grow in waterlogged areas.

Wetlands can be formed by both human activities and natural phenomenon

Threat to wetlands

Wetlands have been lost in the past few years at an alarming rate. Most of them have been drained so that the land they occupy can be built on or cultivated. Some have been filled in as garbage dumps. Many have become polluted. Some peat bogs are being destroyed by large peat-fired power stations.

To save the wetlands, the scientists and conservationists are persuading governments to set aside wetlands for wildlife.

Grasslands

In places with long dry seasons and poor quality soil for most trees, it is mainly grass that grows. These areas are called grasslands. Grasslands are of many different types from the steppe lands of Central Asia to the farmlands of North America.

How are grasslands important ?

Grass is the start of many food chains. It is able to survive nibbling by animals because it sprouts from the bottom, and not from the tips as other plants do. The more the grass is bitten off, the more it grows.

Grass also grows back well after fires, which are common in this ecosystem.

Grasslands provide food for all. There is usually enough to go round because different animals feed on different parts of the grasses, shrubs and trees.

AMAZING FACT !

Insects called termites are a vital part of decomposition in grasslands. They eat dead materials or take it inside their tall mud nests.

Grasslands are rich in food resources and as such are home to various species of animals.

Grasslands all over the world

Grasslands have different names in different parts of the world. There are hot savannahs in East Africa, and veld in Southern Africa. In North America there are the fertile prairies, in South America the dry pampas. The huge areas of grassland in Central Europe and Asia are called steppes, while in western Europe there are meadow and downlands.

Grasslands are known by different names in different countries. In East Africa, they are known as savannahs.

Grasslands are found all across the world

In grasslands different animals feed on different parts of the grasses.

Threat to grasslands

Hunting has drastically reduced the number of grazing animals and their predators on grasslands. Where hunting is banned, people still poach, or hunt illegally. At least 85 per cent of the world's rhinoceroses have been killed by poachers during the last 30 years. Game wardens such as those in Kenya have to look out constantly for hunters. Sometimes they rescue animals that have been illegally trapped.

Forests

A forest is a large area of land covered mainly with trees and undergrowth. Some forests, such as the great Amazon rainforest, have existed for thousands of years. Vast areas of forest have been destroyed by human activity, but others have been planted, and a fifth of the world's land is still covered by forests.

Forests

Forests create their own special environment. At ground level they are generally shady and cool, because the crowns of the trees shield the forest interior from intense heat of the sun. The days are cooler and the nights warmer, making the forest a sheltered place for wildlife.

Forests are home to a large number of animal species

AMAZING FACT !

In the rainforest, the larger trees form an almost continuous canopy over the roof of the forest. A few very tall trees grow through the canopy into the sunlight above.

A tropical rainforest

The importance of forests

Forests have important functions. Like all green plants, trees absorb carbon dioxide from the air, and release oxygen. They help stop the levels of carbon dioxide in the air from rising too high. This is important because high levels of carbon dioxide in the air cause global warming.

A forest acts like a giant sponge, absorbing rainfall and only gradually releasing it into rivers.

Forests help us in countless different ways

Forests provide shelter and food for many animals and produce an enormous range of important products. For large areas of the world, firewood is the main source of energy, the only source that people can afford. Wood is used for house frames, shipbuilding, papermaking, packaging, fencing and many other purposes. The fruits and nuts of forest trees provide food and spices.

Vanishing forests

Each year the world consumes around 3 billion cubic metres of wood. In Britain and much of north-west Europe, human beings have cut down most of trees.

Several rainforests grow on very poor soils. When rainforest is cut down and burned, the remaining soil is often too poor to support crops for long. The soil is easily washed away in the tropical rains, and silts up lakes and reservoirs. The area may even turn to desert.

If forests are cut down at the present rate, around half the world's remaining rainforests will have vanished by the year 2020, with the loss of around one-tenth of all the species on the Earth.

Cutting of trees is a major threat to forests

Atmosphere

The atmosphere is a band of gases known as air surrounding the Earth. It extends from the Earth's surface into outer space. It is made-up of 78 per cent nitrogen, 21 per cent oxygen and 1 per cent other gases.

Importance of atmosphere

Life exists on the Earth mainly because of the atmosphere. It is like a thick blanket covering the Earth and protecting it from the Sun, at the same time providing the necessary conditions in which plants and animals can survive.

Earlier, the Earth had no atmosphere just like most of the other planets today. However, volcanic eruptions on the surface of the Earth produced enough gases to create the atmosphere.

Layers of atmosphere

The atmosphere comprises five major layers : the troposphere, stratosphere, mesosphere, thermosphere, and exosphere. The air gets thinner as you go higher, which is why climbers usually take oxygen cylinder with them when climbing high mountains. The troposphere is the only layer in which living things can breathe normally.

The Earth's atmosphere is composed of air.

AMAZING FACT !

The atmosphere above your head stretches up to 1000 km up. This shows if you could drive a car straight up at 50 km/hour, you would be in space in less than a day.

Troposphere

The lowest layer of the atmosphere is also called the weather layer. This layer contains more than 75 per cent of the atmosphere. In this layer, convection takes place because of which the warm air rises and cold air sinks to fill the space vacated by the former. Clouds occur in this layer and bring rain and snow. The clouds are trapped in the troposphere as the next layer, the stratosphere, is hotter and acts like a lid.

Clouds

A cloud is a mass of tiny water droplets floating in the air, sometimes at a great height from the Earth's surface. Clouds are responsible for different aspects of weather. They give a fair idea as to what the weather will be like in the next few hours or days.

How are clouds formed ?

Clouds are formed from water that has evaporated from oceans, rivers, lakes and from moist soil and plants.
The water is in the form of an invisible gas known as water vapour.
This water vapour forms the clouds, which are actually a collection of tiny water droplets.

When the air near the ground rises into the sky, it cools down and some of its water vapour condenses. These come together to make clouds.

AMAZING FACT !

Smog is a smoky fog formed in cities where the air contains smoke particles released by the industries. Water vapour condenses on these forming smog.

Smog forms over cities with high pollution. It is a smoky fog and is bad for health.

Clouds and Dew

Spider web covered in dew

As we know the clouds form when the water vapour present in the air rises up into the sky, cools down and condenses. The temperature at which this process takes place is known as the dew point.

At this temperature water vapour turns into droplets only if the air contains small particles, like dust and smoke, for it to condense on. If the air is clean, the clouds do not form.

Clouds on earth

Clouds occurring at the ground level are called fog or mist. These clouds are also formed when the air is saturated with water vapour. When the air comes in contact with cold ground, the water vapour condenses. If the distance visible through the cloud is between one and two kilometres, it is known as mist.

Fog is formed when air saturated with water vapour comes in contact with cold ground and condenses.

However, if the distance visible is less than one kilometre, the cloud is known as fog. A dense fog is a very dangerous kind of cloud. It is a hazard to all kinds of transport.

Rain and Snow

Rain and snow are the forms of precipitation by which water is released by the atmosphere. The origin of both of these is the cloud in which tiny drops of water join the cool drops and fall as rain. When ice crystals, instead of water droplets, come down, it results in snowfall.

How does rain form ?

The rain usually starts off as snow even in summers. In the clouds where the temperature is low, ice crystals form. These crystals grow bigger, form snowflakes and fall from the cloud. If the air near the ground is warm, the snow melts and turns into rain. In the tropics, the clouds are warm and so rain is formed when tiny droplets of water in the clouds collide and join together. When the drops are heavy enough, they fall as rain. In thinner clouds, few drops collide making smaller rain drops. These kinds of rain drops are called drizzle.

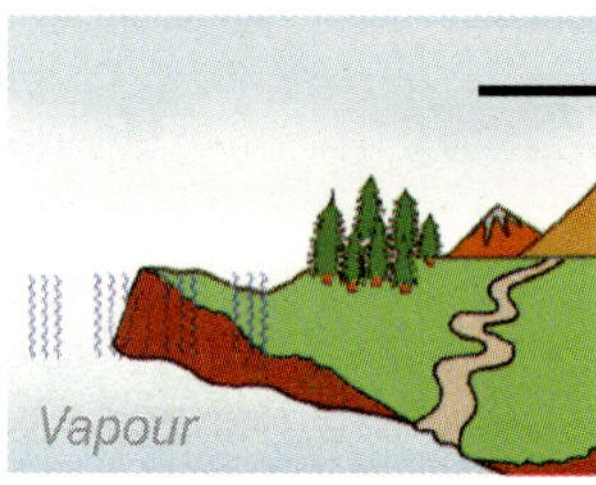

Water is evaporated by solar heat and forms vapour in the air.

Warmer weather causes water vapour to rise and meet cold air in the sky. Water vapour condenses back into water droplets and forms clouds.

When more of the vapour turns to droplets, the clouds grow bigger and darker.

The droplets grow too large to be held in the air so they fall down as rain drops.

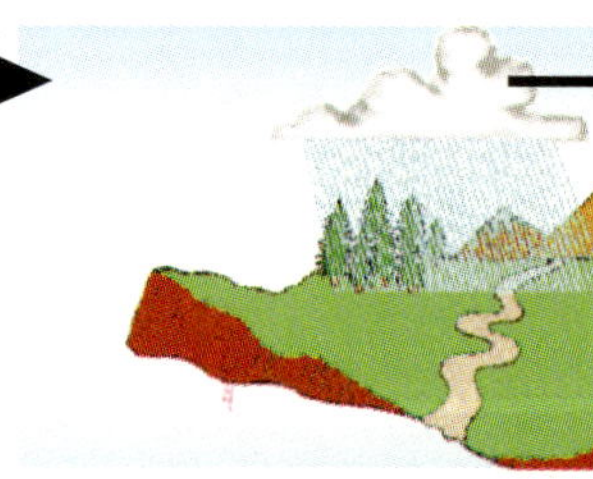

When clouds could no longer hold moisture, it starts raining.

The rain cycle is an ongoing process.

How does snow form ?

As discussed earlier, ice crystals are formed in clouds where the temperature is below the freezing point. To form snowflakes, the crystals join together as they fall and become wet, and then re-freeze. When they precipitate, they fall on the ground as snowflakes only if the temperature of the air surrounding the ground is below freezing point.

Snow consists of tiny crystals of ice. Every snow crystal is different from the others.

Snowflakes are actually a collection of ice crystals comprising frozen water vapour. No two snowflakes are exactly alike. Ice crystals are divided into as many as 80 categories.

AMAZING FACT !

Snow is white and not pink. But in Greenland, pink snow is found. It is the red algae living inside that gives the snow its pink colour.

Snow that never melts

Ice caps and glaciers are actually made-up of snow that never melts. Here, all the ice crystals and snowflakes squeeze together by the weight of more snow falling from the sky.

Ice crystals and snowflakes squeeze together to form never melting ice. Ice caps and glaciers are made-up of these.

Ice caps and glaciers usually form on the tops of the mountains and near the poles.

Snowflakes

Wind and Storm

Wind is the movement of air which depends upon variations in atmospheric pressure. Air normally flows from areas of high atmospheric pressure to areas of low atmospheric pressure. The speed of the wind depends on the differences in the air pressures.

How are winds formed ?

Winds are formed when there is a difference in the air pressure and temperature between one place and another.

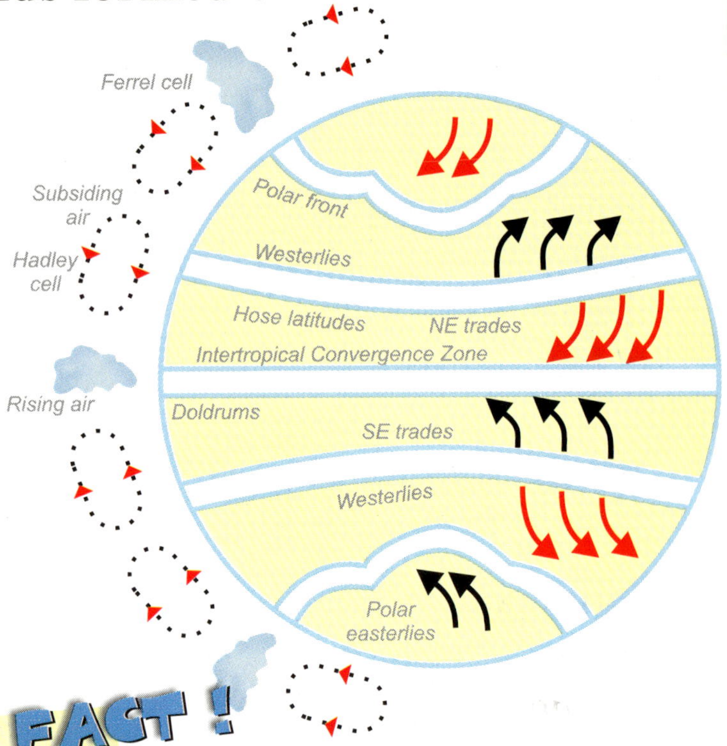

The three-cell general circulation model of the atmosphere

AMAZING FACT !

The world's highest air temperature, 58°C, was recorded in the Sahara Desert in Libya, Africa, in 1922.

Winds flow from areas of high pressure to the areas of low pressure.

When air is warmer, it is less dense than cold air and rises up into the sky creating a low pressure area. The cold air sinks down to the Earth and moves in to fill the space vacated by the warm air. This circulation of air gives birth to the winds.

Wind generator

An aerial view of a collapsed thunderstorm

Thunderstorms

Thunderclouds are created when inside the clouds, some of the water freezes and strong air currents force the ice and water droplets collide together.
This collision leads to separation of electrons from some droplets and formation of positive and negative charges in the cloud. This charge is liberated by lightning.
The lightning heats the air surrounding it which results in the expansion of air. This expansion is faster than the speed of sound and results in the peal of thunder.

Hurricanes and tornadoes

Hurricanes are the tropical cyclones that are violent enough to flatten buildings. Hurricanes start to form when the Sun's heat stirs up moist air over the oceans where the temperature is high.
At the centre of the hurricanes there is a ring of low pressure called the eye. A huge column of hot and moist air develops around it. As this air moves round and cools, the water inside condenses into rain.

The winds in a hurricane spiral around the eye, a central calm area of low pressure.

Tornadoes are small and extremely violent whirlwinds that form when a long funnel of warm air stretches up from the ground. As the tornado moves, it sucks up everything that it comes across.

In a tornado, a funnel-shaped cloud is formed which causes great destruction as it passes.

Seasons

The Sun pours out energy in various directions and the seasons and climate depend on this energy. As each season arrives the length of daylight and the daily weather change. Summer days are longer and warmer while the winter days are shorter and cooler.

How do season occur ?

The occurrence of seasons depends on Earth orbiting the Sun. As we know that the spinning Earth always tilts at a definite angle and takes 365.26 days to go round the Sun once. When the Earth is on one side of its orbit, the tilt bends the northern hemisphere towards the Sun. After six months, when the Earth is on the other side of its orbit, the southern hemisphere bends towards the Sun. The hemisphere leaning towards the Sun experiences summer while the other hemisphere experiences winters.

Summer

Winter

AMAZING FACT !

At Christmas, the countries of northern hemisphere face harsh winters while the countries in southern hemisphere face summer hot enough for a dip in the sea.

Rain

The changing daylengths

The length of the day changes during the year except at places close to the equator, where the days are 12 hours long every day of the year. Day and night lengths are equal everywhere in the world on two equinoxes, around 21 March and 23 September.

The length of daylight changes during the year in all parts of the world.

Usually, it is longest at midsummer and shortest at midwinter. The daylength affects the behaviour of all plants and animals: birds lay their eggs in spring and not all plants flowers at the same time of the year.

The difference in day length depends on the tilt of Earth's axis and also the latitude. The midnight Sun occurs at latitudes greater than 67° North or South at midsummer.

Midnight Sun

Close to the North and South Poles, there are places where the Sun never sets for days or weeks in midsummer. These places experience the Midnight Sun. In midwinter, the opposite happens and the Sun never rises.

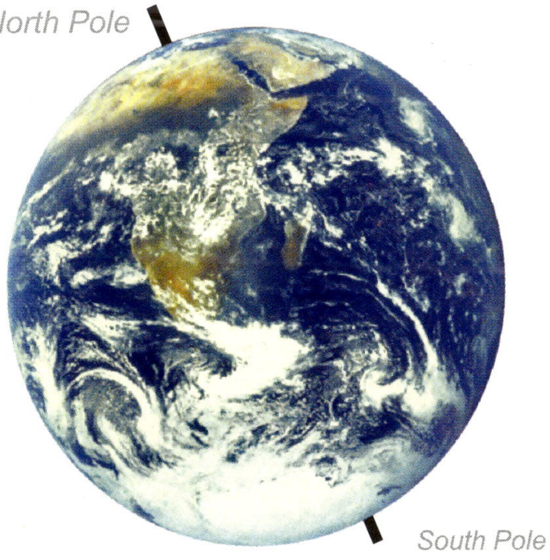

In polar regions, the Sun never sets in midsummer. While in midwinter, the Sun never rises.

This effect happens because the Earth's axis is tilted. The places that get the Midnight Sun lie inside the Arctic and Antarctic circles. The Antarctic has no permanent inhabitants, but people living near and inside the Arctic Circle have to adapt to long periods of continuous daylight or night-time.

Climate

The climate of a particular region of the world describes the average weather conditions over a long period of time. These conditions include the average temperature, rainfall, air pressure, humidity, and wind speed and direction in that region.

Factors determining the climate

Temperature and rainfall are the most important factors determining the climate. Warm air holds far more water than cold air. Close to the equator, air is warmed by the Sun and holds a lot of water evaporated from the oceans. As it rises, the water condenses into clouds and falls as rain so this area tends to be hot and wet.

Dry, sandy deserts are often intensely hot by day and cold by night.

In the polar regions, the Sun's rays must travel much further through the air before reaching the ground and lose a lot of the Sun's warmth on the way. These are the coldest parts of the world.

Polar regions have the most severe climate in the world.

Climate zones

The Earth can be roughly divided into six climatic zones. Within each zone there are variations due to altitude and latitude.

Polar climate : Always cold, brief chilly summer, little rain or snowfall.

Mountain climate : Affected by altitude, cooler and wetter that the climates of neighbouring areas.

Cold forest climate : Short, cool summer and long, cold winter, light to moderate rainfall.

Mid-latitude climate: Moderately warm summer and mild, cool winter, average temperature, moderate rainfall in all seasons.

Dry climate : Hot to cold, great changes in daily temperature except in coastal areas, little rainfall.

Tropical rainy climate: Always hot and wet, heavy rainfall throughout the year.

AMAZING FACT !

Major volcanic eruptions are a possible cause of climate change. They add large amounts of ash and gases into the upper atmosphere.

The changing climate

The world's climate has been changing slowly over many hundreds or thousands of years. Scientists believe that there are many natural reasons for climate change. These include long term changes in the Earth's orbit around the Sun, and variations in the amount of the Sun's heat that reaches the Earth's surface. Climate is also affected by human activity. By burning large amounts of fossil, fuels, we are releasing increased amounts of carbon dioxide into the atmosphere.

Studying the Earth

A map is a means of depicting on a two-dimensional flat surface the size, shape and features of a three dimensional tract of land. A map is capable of giving us a glance of the whole world. Without a map, it would be very difficult to get an idea of the Earth.

Making a map

To make a map, it is necessary to carry out an accurate survey of an area of land. Today map making is aided by aerial photography and surveys from satellites. Atlas maps are small scale maps that show large areas with little detail. The scale of a map can be shown by a scale line or bar. This is divided up to show what distances on the map mean on the ground. Maps may be drawn to different scales.

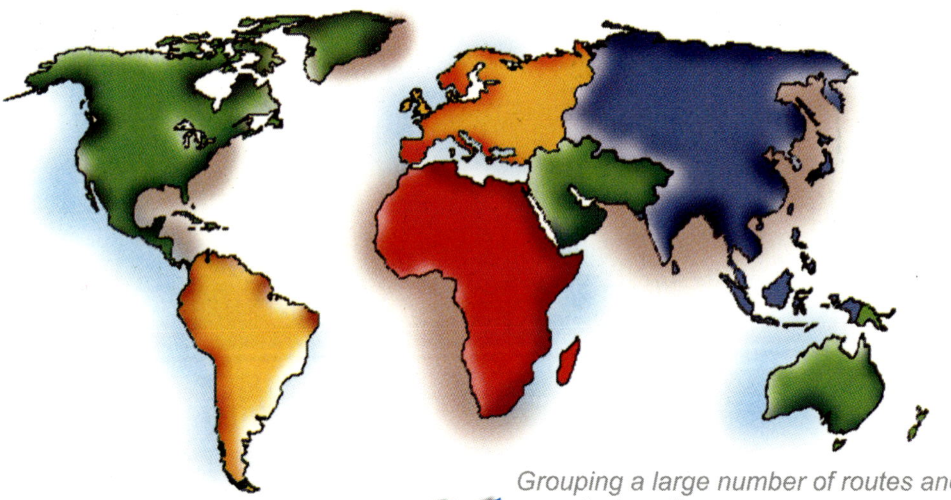

Grouping a large number of routes and their outlines creates a map.

AMAZING FACT !

A relief map is a scaled-down, three-dimensional model of the land's surface features, or relief. It gives an idea what the land's hills, valleys and vegetation may look like.

Before maps were invented people directed each other by landmarks. Maps were invented by painstakingly tracing each route taken from one point to the other.

AMAZING FACT !

Maps do not show everything. Therefore before using a map outdoors, it is helpful to turn it so that it faces north. This is called setting or orientating the map.

Kinds of maps

There are various different kinds of maps such as physical maps, political maps and topographic maps. Physical maps show the natural features of an area of land such as hills and rivers.

Political maps include countries and their boundaries, capital cities and some times other towns or administrative areas. Topographic maps shows the physical features together with human features like towns, roads and country boundaries.

Gerardus Mercator

A map projection is used to portray all or a part of the round Earth on a flat surface. This cannot be done without some distortion. For example, the basic Mercator projection is unique; it yields the only map on which a straight line drawn anywhere within its bounds shows a particular type of direction, but distances and areas are grossly distorted near the map's polar regions. It was introduced by Geradus Mercator in 1569.

Fossils

Fossils are the remains of plants and animals that have been preserved in rocks. A fossil may be any remain or trace, such as a shell, bone or a foot print preserved in a rock by gradually being changed into rock itself.

How do fossils form?

Fossils form when animal or plant remains get covered with sediments that later turn into rock. When an organism dies its body comes to rest on the bottom of a lake or the sea.

Fossilized insect trapped in an amber millions of years ago.

The soft parts of the body such as the skin and the muscles decay leaving the hard parts such as the bones of skeleton behind.

These parts are covered with mud and sand and gradually these sediments turn into rock. After millions of years the landscape changes, and if the rock containing the fossils rises and is worn away, the fossil can be seen.

AMAZING FACT !

Tyrannosaurus was one of the biggest flesh-eating animals that has ever lived, and was probably one of the last dinosaurs to evolve. It measured about 12m in length.

Fossilized dinosaurs skeleton

Studying the fossils

Various kinds of researches and studies conducted on fossils give us a fair idea as to what were the organisms living in past like. Today, everything that we know about dinosaurs has been learned from fossils.

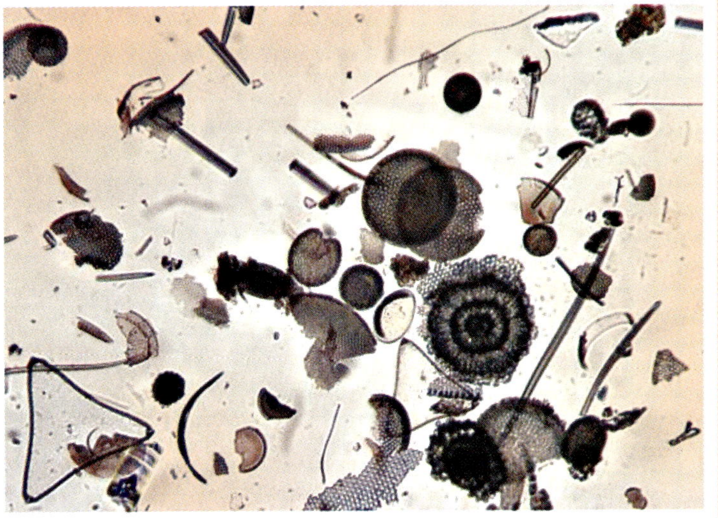

Diatom plant fossils viewed through a microscope

If scientists discover a new kind of dinosaur, they study its bones to work out the shape of its body and how it walked and ran, and what other kinds of dinosaur it is related to. The position in which some dinosaur fossils have been found tells us that certain kinds of dinosaurs lived in herds.

Fossil fuels

Fossil fuel is the name given to fuels, which are extracted from the rocks of the Earth's crust. They are used to provide the fuel for heating and the generation of power such as electricity. Many chemicals are also derived from these fuels, which are made from the animal and plant remains that have formed fossils, hence their name. - The fossil fuels.

Some of the commonly found fossils fuels include coal, petroleum and natural gas.

Coal can be extracted from seams that lie near the surface by removing the topsoil to make an open-cast pit.

Soil

Soil is a mixture of differently sized fragments of rocks and minerals, together with plant and animal debris, water, air, soil animals and plants. The soil is the surface layer of the Earth, beneath which lies the broken rock, the subsoil and then bedrock.

Importance of soil

Soil is essential for the growth of plants which in turn are responsible for the existence of life on Earth. Soil contains a dark organic material called humus that is composed of dead plants. It retains moisture and provides the nutrients essential for the growth of the new plants. The roots of plants push through the soil creating air spaces, enabling animals and bacteria to live in the soil.

Soil supports the growth of plants which are indispensable for the existence of life on Earth.

A healthy soil is a balance of minerals, humus, bacteria, soil animals, air and water.

AMAZING FACT !

Soils differ in the sizes of the tiny particles that make them up. In sandy soil, the particles are comparatively large while in clay soil, the particles are very small.

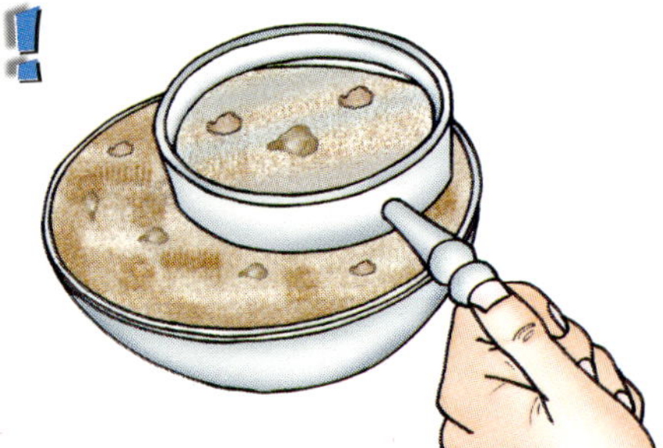

A magnifying glass clearly shows particles of larger soil in sand.

Soil profile

Soil is formed in a number of layers. Their sequence is called the soil profile. The layers, also called horizons, show the different things that go into making a soil – from the decay of rocks to the addition of material from living things.

Not all soils have the same horizons, and their sizes vary from soil to soil. Topsoil, which holds the roots of most small plants, is the uppermost layer. Below it is the subsoil, which overlies fragmented rock on top of bedrock. The upper layers contain humus, used by plants for food, which is formed by the decay of organic matter.

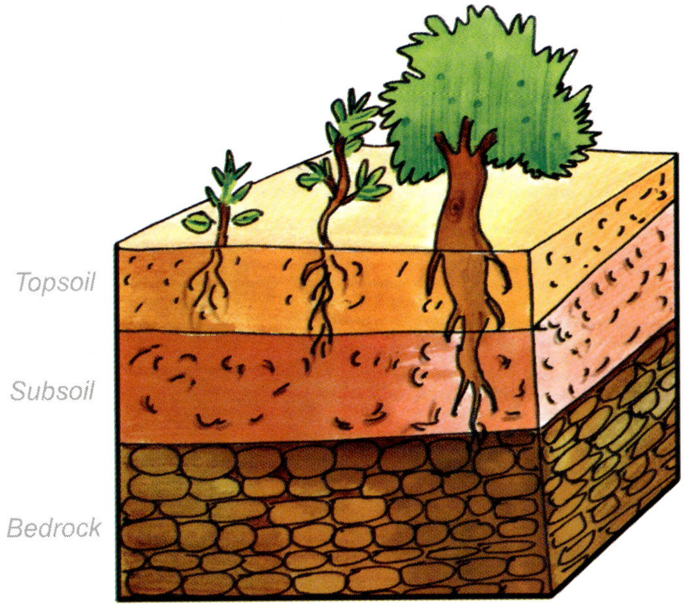

Topsoil which holds the roots of plants is the uppermost layer. Below it is the subsoil, which overlies fragmented rock on top of bedrock.

Soil often erodes by the action of heavy winds and running water.

Soil erosion

Erosion comes from the Latin word meaning 'to gnaw'. The rocky surface of the Earth is being slowly worn away by the action of water, wind and Sun.
Tiny pieces of rock are then carried away by water and wind and deposited in other places, especially in the sea. This process is called erosion. Soil erosion affects the composition of the soil.
It blows or washes away the top layer of the soil which supports the growth of plants.

Living on Earth

Our home planet, Earth, is a unique planet. Amongst all the nine planets in the solar system, Earth is the only one that supports life. This is because Earth has everything upon which living organisms can thrive.

Right temperature

Our planet Earth is located at the correct distance from the Sun. It is neither too hot nor too cold. On all other planets, life cannot exist because they do not offer the appropriate temperature.

Planets like Mercury and Venus are too close to the Sun and hence very hot. On the other hand, other planets like Jupiter, Saturn and Pluto are very cold and dark. So life cannot exist on these planets.

AMAZING FACT !

The atmosphere of Jupiter is a thick layer which contains methane and ammonia. One landing on Jupiter would actually sink through its atmosphere.

Earth has all the conditions required for the existence of life.

Water

Earth is also called the blue planet as the presence of plenty of water gives it a blue appearance. About 71 per cent of the total surface of Earth is covered with water.

Water is indispensable for life. It also plays a crucial role in determining the climates all over the world. Other planets are devoid of water and hence cannot support life.

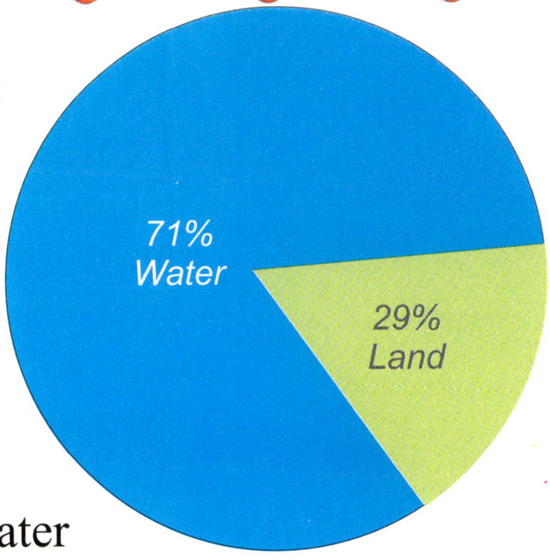

Earth has sufficient quantity of water which supports different forms of life.

Atmosphere acts like a blanket that covers the Earth and absorbs harmful radiations.

Atmosphere

The atmosphere makes it possible for us to live on Earth. It consists of layers of air that surround our planet.

It is wrapped around the Earth rather like orange peel and is a mixture of gases, mainly nitrogen and oxygen.

Other planets also have atmospheres but these are very different. On Venus, the air is thick with carbon dioxide which traps the Sun's heat raising temperatures to 480ºC which is too hot for life to exist.

The atmosphere on Mars is very thin because of which Sun's heat bounces away and temperatures fall to –120ºC. Conditions on the Earth is in between those on Mars and Venus.

Earth in Danger

Today Earth is facing many environmental problems. These problems are caused by human activities. People need food and water, space to live, air to breathe and energy to drive machines. This leaves less space and food for plants and animals.

Pollution

Pollution is one of the major environmental problems that the Earth is facing today. Pollution is caused by evil human practices.

Smoke liberated by the factories and vehicles pollute the environment and adversely affect life on Earth. Factory wastes pollute rivers and lakes, killing the wildlife.

Pollution is one of the major environmental problems that further leads to many other problems.

Global warming

When we burn oil, coal, and wood, we release carbon dioxide into the atmosphere. All this extra carbon dioxide is creating a 'blanket' around the Earth. Most of the long-wave heat radiation from Earth cannot escape, causing the Earth to get hotter and hotter. This is called the 'greenhouse effect' and causes global warming.

Carbon dioxide leads to the greenhouse effect which in turn causes global warming.

AMAZING FACT !

Fumes from traffic are responsible for releasing more than 225,000 tonnes of lead into the atmosphere every year.

Acid rain

Poisonous gases from power stations and vehicles mix with water in the air. This then falls as acid rain and becomes part of the water cycle. Acid in the rain can damage wildlife in all ecosystems where it falls. It also affects stone, causing statues and buildings to crumble away.

Acid rain adversely affects buildings, vegetation and wildlife.

Save Earth 

With the need to provide housing and food for more and more people there is less space for other living things. Conservation is the action to stop rare animals and plants from dying out and to stop common animals and plants from becoming rare. It also aims at protecting the wild places where all these animals and plants live.

What is environmental conservation?

Conservation is the management of the environment, in all aspects, in such a way that its quality and natural resources are maintained.

It does not necessarily mean that particular forms of wildlife, habitats or climates, for example, should be protected and preserved unchanging forever.

Conservation recognizes that any natural systems is constantly changing. Although humans evolved as part of the Earth's natural environment, our activities are often very damaging on a large scale.

It is, therefore, necessary for humans to manage the environment, and the effects they have upon it, wisely.

Plantation of trees and proper dumping of waste products are easy solutions to various environmental problems.

Solutions to environmental problems

These problems can be solved by banning hunting, protecting habitats, setting up nature reserves and reducing pollution. People have now become very concerned about environmental problems. Organizations, such as the Worldwide Fund for Nature (WWF), and the International Union for the Conservation of Nature and Natural Resources (IUCN), make people aware of problems and raise money to protect species and habitats.

AMAZING FACT !

The Yellowstone National Park in the United States was the world's first National Park.

Wildlife sanctuaries are meant for protecting the endangered species of animals.

What we can do ?

We all can give our contribution in protecting the environment. We can collect paper, tins and bottles for recycling. This will reduce the number of trees cut down and mines dug under rare habitats. We can also stop buying things made from rare plants and animals and avoid using non-biodegradable packaging.

Unit – 4

The World of Animals

Evolution 

Evolution is the way new kinds of plants, animals and other living things come into being as a result of many small changes over a long period of time. Evolution of life began more than 3,500 million years ago.

Evidence of fossils

Evidences from fossils in ancient rocks show that over millions of years new kinds of creature have appeared. At the same time some of the old forms such as the dinosaurs, have become extinct.

An 'ancient wing' bird known as Archaeopteryx.

Darwin's theory

Darwin's theory of evolution can explain the development of the pterosaur, an ancient flying reptile that lived over 150 million years ago. It began as a four-footed lizard. Over millions of years, small folds of skin developed between its feet, which enabled it to glide from tree to tree. Over many more generations, the folds and the bones and muscles supporting them formed wings.

Hyracotherium the 'dawn horse' lived over 500 million years ago.

Mesohippus the 'middle horse' lived 300 million years ago.

The first mammals and birds

Most reptiles were heavy-bodied and slow-moving, but a few developed in such a way that they were able to move faster and so escape from predators (hunting animals). Changes in their skull and their ribs suggest that they breathed regularly, like mammals. The first true mammals had developed from these mammal-like reptiles by the time of the earliest dinosaurs.

Birds evolved later. The earliest bird that we know, lived about 147 million years ago. It was clearly related to small flesh-eating dinosaurs.

When the dinosaurs died about 65 million years ago, mammals, birds and modern types of fishes and flowering plants survived. In a relatively short period of time huge numbers of mammals and birds occupied much of the land and the seas. Eventually the mammals were left as the largest living creatures.

AMAZING FACT !

Ninety-nine per cent of all the different kinds of animal that have ever lived are now extinct.

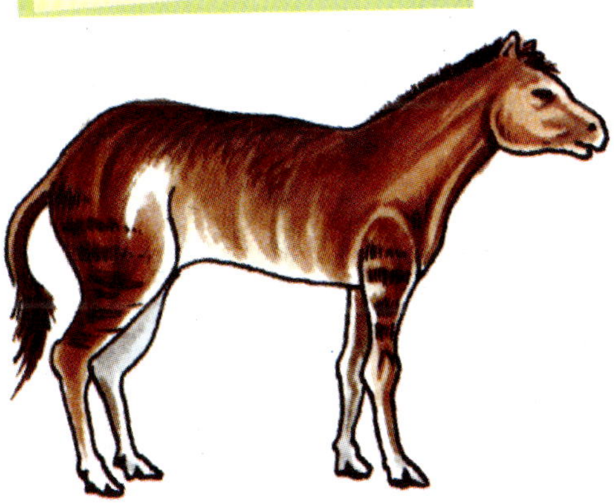

Merychippus appeared around 20 million years ago. It was the first horse to eat grass.

Equus, the modern horse evolved around 2 million years ago. It lives on grass and has just a single toe on each foot.

Classifying Living Things

The animal kingdom can be classified into two groups: vertebrates (animals with backbones) and invertebrates (animals without backbones). Scientists have probably identified most kinds of vertebrates, but there may be millions of invertebrates that they have not identified.

Vertebrates and invertebrates

The word 'vertebrate' comes from the Latin word for a backbone, so vertebrates are animals with backbones. There are five major groups of vertebrates: fishes, amphibians, reptiles, birds, and mammals.

Almost all the bigger, more complicated animals are vertebrates, but there are many more different kinds of invertebrates – animals without backbones. These include insects, squids, snails, jellyfishes, and worms. Invertebrates do not have bones but may be supported by some kind of hard shell outside or inside their body.

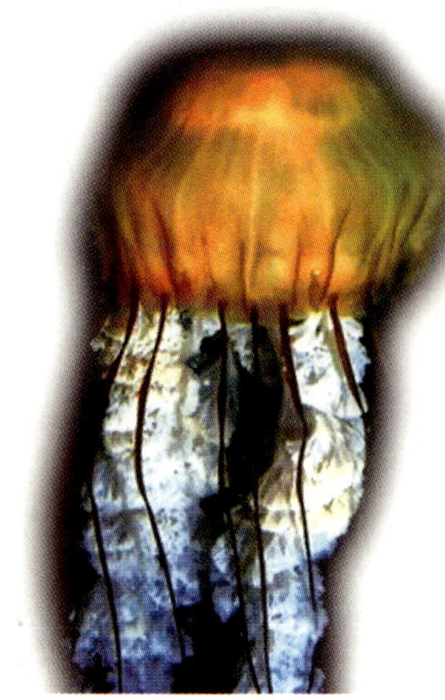

Jellyfish is an invertebrate.

AMAZING FACT !

The fastest land animal is the Cheetah, which can run, for a short distance at up to 100 km/h.

Cheetah

Mammals

Mammals are found almost everywhere in the world. There are about 4,000 different kinds of mammals. Mammals are vertebrates and are more intelligent than other animals.

Lion is a mammal.

Snake is a reptile.

Reptiles

Reptiles are also backboned animals and they breathe through lungs. Crocodiles, tortoises, snakes and lizards, all fall in the category of reptiles.

Amphibians

Amphibians are vertebrates and most have moist and soft skins. Amphibians are animals that start their lives in water and change as they grow up, so they are able to live on land as well.

Frog is an amphibian.

Parrots are birds.

Birds

Birds are also vertebrates and are warm blooded animals. These creatures have feathers and wings and lay eggs on land. This class of animals can fly in the sky.

Insects

Insects are all invertebrates. They do not have backbones to support their skeleton.

Ladybird

Single-celled Organisms

Single-celled organisms are the ones that have a single eukaryotic cell. Wet places such as the sea, ponds and damp ground are full of tiny single celled organisms. These organisms are called protists. They are bigger than bacteria, most are still far too small to be seen with the naked eye.

Bacteria

Bacteria are very simple living things, consisting of a single cell. They are found everywhere: in the ocean depths, in soil, on our skins, even floating freely in the air.

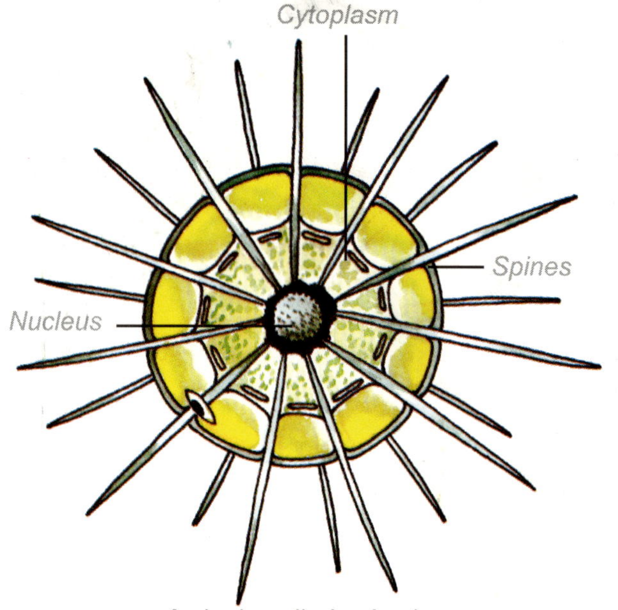

A single-celled animal

They are some of the oldest living things, and fossils have been found of bacteria that lived 3,000 million years ago.

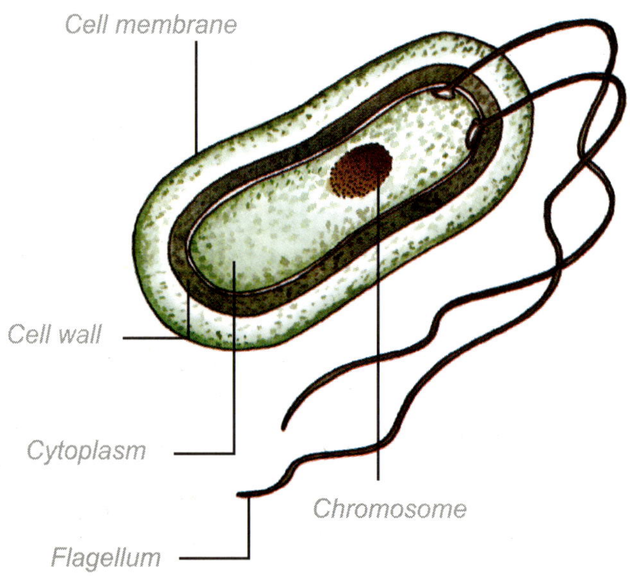

A bacterium

Some bacteria can make their own food by using the Sun's energy (photosynthesis), but most live on decaying plants and animals.

Viruses

Viruses are made up of a coating of proteins around the material needed for reproduction (genetic material). They can only reproduce by entering the nucleus of a living cell and inserting their genetic material into the genetic material of the cell.

Unlike bacteria, viruses cannot be killed by antibiotics. But it is possible to be vaccinated against many diseases caused by viruses.

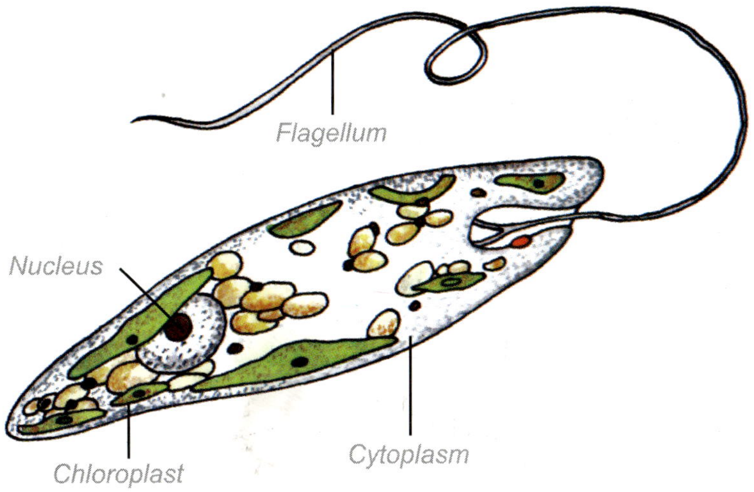

A single celled aquatic animal

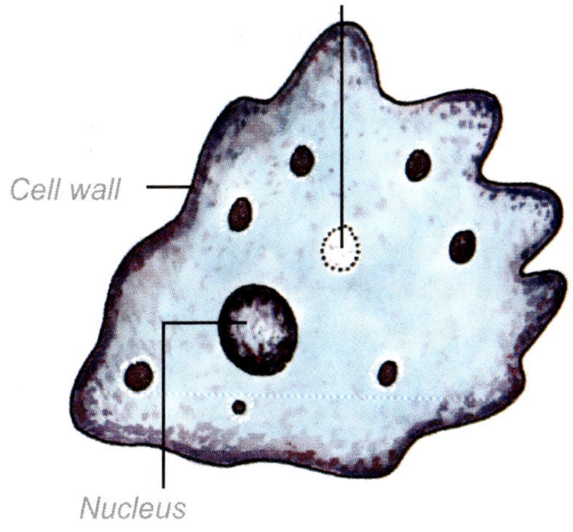

An amoeba, a microscopic single-celled animal.

AMAZING FACT !

An infected mosquito has plasmodium cell in its salivary glands. These can enter a human when the mosquito bites.

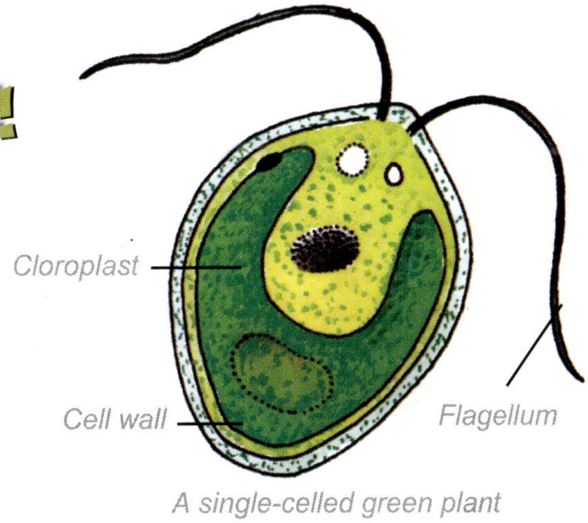

A single-celled green plant

Introduction to Fish 

Fishes are cold-blooded animals with backbones, gills and fins. They all live in water and can be found in ponds, lakes and rivers, and in the sea. Most sea-dwelling fishes live in the shallows close to land and in the surface waters of the great oceans.

The life of a fish

Blue fish

Most fishes are born from eggs, although a few kinds are born alive. Usually fishes have a definite breeding season. Some, like eels and salmon, migrate long distances to reach the best place to spawn (produce eggs). In most fishes the females lay huge numbers of eggs. These are almost always fertilized by the male outside the female's body. It is unusual for fishes to take care of their young.

How do fishes swim ?

When they swim, most fishes use powerful muscles which move their bodies and tails from side to side. Fishes do not sink in the water even when they are totally still. Most of the fishes have an internal swim bladder, a gas-filled bag which holds them up. When they swim, all their energy goes into pushing forward through the water.

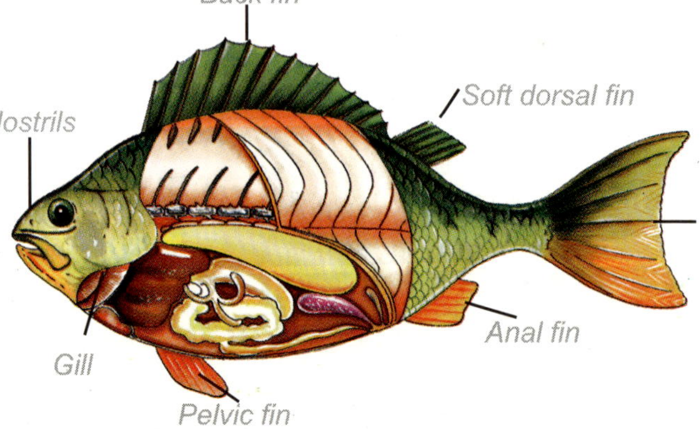

The senses of a fish

Fishes have the same basic senses as we do: sight, hearing, touch, smell and taste. Most fishes have eyes on the sides of their heads, which gives them all-round vision. Many fishes have good colour vision. This is important in the courtship of some species, while others that can change their colour to match their surroundings. Fishes' ears are inside their skull. They work as organs of balance as well as of hearing.

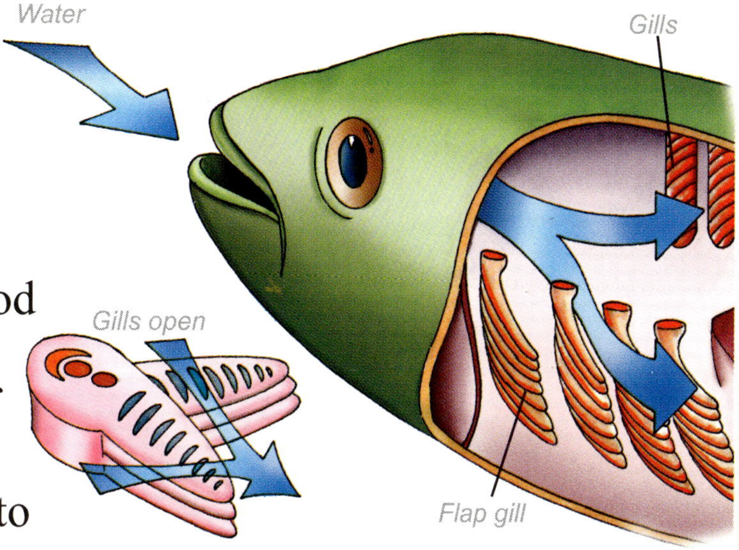

Fish breathe through special structure known as gill at the sides of the head. Gills are made up of large numbers of delicate plates, packed with blood vessels.

Many fishes live where there is little light, so their sense of touch is important. A fish's main organ of touch are its 'lateral lines'. Most fishes have a very good sense of smell. Many use smell to find their prey. The sense of taste is related to the sense of smell. Some fishes have large numbers of taste buds in and around the mouth.

Angelfish

AMAZING FACT !

Almost half the 43,000 species of animals with backbones (vertebrates) are fishes. Some of the species that have evolved are very strange indeed.

Sharks and Rays

Sharks and rays are different from other kinds of fish. The main difference is that their skeletons are made-up of cartilages and not of bones. Other distinguishing feature is that the gills open externally through a series of gill slits.

Shark

Shark is cartilaginous fish of marine and fresh waters. Sharks have a skeleton formed entirely of cartilage rather than bone. Reproduction in sharks is by internal fertilization, unlike that of bony fishes. The body is spindle-shaped, and the upper part of the tail is usually better developed than the lower half. Sharks swim by winding movements of the whole body, there is no swim bladder, so they must swim constantly to avoid sinking. All sharks are extremely good swimmers and active predators. Only 27 of 250 species of sharks have been definitely implicated in attacks on humans. A flesh-eating shark may have up to 3,000 teeth, but most of them are located behind the front row of teeth.

Sharks are powerful fish with jagged triangular teeth. These teeth help them to kill their prey easily.

AMAZING FACT !

Sharks can detect electric currents in the water, which means they can trace prey by the electricity made in their body.

Ray

The ray is a flat-bodied fish with a boneless skeleton made from a tough, elastic substance called cartilage. It has mouth and gill openings on the underside, a slender tail and cylindrical, dorsal and tail fins. The largest known ray is the manta ray, which may grow to 7m wide and weigh up to 1,360 kg.

Manta ray

Devil ray

Devil Ray

Devil ray is a giant ray widespread in surface waters of tropical and warm temperate seas. Its pectoral fins form large triangular wings. It has a body width up to 6 m and sides of its head prolonged as fleshy 'horns', its tail is whip-like. Young are born alive, feed on plankton and small fishes.

Electric Ray

The electric ray belongs to the family of sluggish, bottom-living marine rays, widespread in tropical to temperate seas. Its body is disc shaped, skin smooth, tail robust. Its well-developed electric organs produce strong shocks to stun prey. Also called torpedo rays, electric rays include large North Atlantic species, *Torpedo nobiliana*, which measure up to 1.8m in length.

Eagle ray

Electric ray

Amphibians 

Amphibians are animals that start their lives in water and change as they grow up, so they are able to live on land as well. All of them are vertebrates and have moist and soft skins.

Kinds of amphibians

There are three main kinds of amphibians. Blindworms are one kind that have no legs and a grooved skin, like earthworms. Newts and salamanders resemble lizards. They are often brightly coloured. Frogs and toads are the most common amphibians known to mankind. They don't have tails, but have long, powerful hind legs. These legs help them swim as well as jump.

Earthworm

AMAZING FACT !

Blindworms are unusual amphibians because only one species lives in water.

Newt

Salamander

Frog

Newts and Salamanders

Newts and Salamanders have long narrow bodies, long tails and short legs with webbed feet for swimming. They use their powerful tails to propel themselves through water. They feed on worms and insects and use their tongues to catch the prey. Many of them spend their adult lives on land, but a few live mainly in water. Many of them produce poisonous slime from glands in their skin. They may be brightly coloured to warn enemies of their poison.

Salamander

Newt

Newts and salamanders are a kind of amphibians that have long bodies with small or no legs.

AMAZING FACT !

The word 'amphibian' comes from the Greek words amphibios and means 'both ways of life'.

Frogs and Toads

Both of them are good swimmers and on land most move about by leaping in a zig-zag pattern. Many are active mainly at night. They have small lungs, but they also breathe partly through their moist, soft skins. If their skin were to dry out, they would suffocate. Toads usually have drier skins than frogs. They catch their prey with long, sticky tongues, others leap and grab insects in their mouths..

Toad

Frog

Both frogs and toads are very similar in appearance. They have long back legs, webbed toes and no tail.

Snakes

Snakes are reptiles that have no legs. A number of snakes are burrowers, but most live on ground. A few climb into trees or even live in the sea.

How do snakes move ?

Many snakes move by throwing their bodies into curves that push against any unevenness in the ground. These snakes cannot move on smooth surfaces. Snakes are not slimy creatures. Their skin is dry and scaly. After regular intervals they shed their outer skin. This process is known as 'sloughing' and the skin is know as 'slough'.

A snake's body is so flexible that it can easily move in any direction.

AMAZING FACT !

During mating, the males often compete with each other or put on displays for females. After mating, most female snakes lay eggs, although some give birth to live young.

Eating habits of snakes

All the snakes are flesh-eaters. They track their prey using their long, forked tongues, which flicker over the ground. The tongue picks up tiny traces of scent left by animals. Grass snakes, catch their food by grabbing and swallowing it.

Mamba

Others like python, often called constrictors, loop their prey and suffocate it. Almost all the snakes paralyse their prey using their poison. Snakes usually swallow their whole food and have distinct bulge in their bodies after eating.

Different snakes

There are a variety of snakes found on Earth. A few of them are python, boomslangs, viper, cobra, anaconda, etc.

Anaconda

Python is a snake bearing small spurs as the vestiges of hind limbs. Its body has bold colour patterns in browns and yellows.

The largest species, the reticulate python of Asia, is 11m long; they feed on small mammals, birds, reptiles and frogs. Vipers are short, stoutly built and typically terrestial. Cobra is another snake that is really very poisonous. If its venom (poison) enters the eye of a person, he can go blind. The king cobra is the longest of all poisonous snakes, with length of 6m. Anaconda is the largest snake with length of 9 m and 100 cm in circumference. It is not poisonous but kills by constriction.

Cobra

Python

Lizards 

Lizards are small reptiles. Many of them live in warmer and drier regions of the world and can often be seen sunning themselves or scuttling away from danger.

Characteristics of lizards

Lizards have sharp eyesight and a good sense of hearing. They usually feed on insects and other small animals. Some of them are burrowers, hunting their prey underground.

House lizard

Frilled lizard

Their skin is silky smooth and their legs are small. A few, such as slow-worms, have no legs at all.

House lizards

Usually, lizards avoid humans, but gecko is the creature that lives in buildings. They have fine hair pads on their feet which help them to climb walls or walk upside-down on ceilings. Common wall lizards are also welcomed in houses, as they kill the enemies of humans, flies and mosquitoes.

Leaf-tailed gecko

Chameleons

Chameleons are small lizards that have a very special kind of camouflage. They change colour in less than two minutes, whenever they feel danger around them. They can change their colours according to their surroundings. For instance, if a chameleon is on a leaf or on a tree, it will change its colour to green. And if it is on the trunk of a tree, it will transform from green to brown.

In bright sunshine they are a rich green, while at night they become whiter. A frightened chameleon may turn pale, while an angry one goes blackish green.

Chameleons can not only change their colour but also their textures accordingly.

AMAZING FACT !

The largest lizard is the Komodo dragon, which grows to over 3m long and weighs over 100 kg.

When a chameleon is close enough to its prey, it judges its position with its round eyes and takes aim. It traps the insects on the sticky pad of its tongue and eats it.

Know About Birds

Bird is an animal adapted for flight and unique in its body covering of feathers. There are more than 8,500 species of birds. They are regarded as the descendants of reptiles of the dinosaur group. They reproduce by laying eggs that must be kept warm for correct development.

We can see birds in all parts of the world. They can be found in rainforests, oceans and deserts. Most birds can soar up in the sky, while penguins may dive to a depth of over 250 metres. The eating habits vary from bird to bird. Some of them eat only plants and some feed on only fresh meat.

Birds are warm-blooded animals. They are the only animals that can fly high in the sky. Their feathers enable them to fly. Their bodies are specially designed to help them fly efficiently. Although a few birds such as penguins and kiwis are not able to fly.

Penguins and kiwis are flightless bird.

Flight

The bones of the birds are very light in weight and are hollow. In the breeding season females lay eggs periodically. The young ones grow in a nest so that the mother is not weighed down by carrying them.

All birds do not fly in the same manner. Big birds like, gulls, often glide, and vultures hardly move their wings as they soar for hours on end. Some birds like, kestrels, can fly in the air as they look for prey on the ground. White peregrines, which hunt other birds, can reach up to the speed of 180 km/h. Starlings fly in a straight line, moving their wings all the time. Woodpeckers close their wings between flaps and 'bound' along.

Birds are able to fly because their bones are light and hollow.

Feathers

Feathers cover almost all parts of a bird's body, They are made by the bird's skin, in much the same way that our skin makes hair or fingernails. Usually, only a bird's beak, eyes, legs and feet remain bare. Feathers have three other important functions. First, they are very good for keeping the bird dry and warm. In cold weather birds fluff up their feathers so that layers of insulating air is trapped between them. Shapes of the secondary wing feathers help provide the lift that keeps a flying bird in the air. The third important function of feathers is to give birds a streamlined shape, which also helps birds in flight. Feathers can also be used for camouflage, because birds need to stay hidden while sitting on their eggs. Males are often showy and brightly coloured in order to attract a females.

AMAZING FACT !

The Arctic tern has the longest migration route of any animal. Including the return trip, it can cover a distance of over 35,000 km in a year.

Male birds are more brightly coloured and attractive than female birds.

Game Birds and Sea Birds 

As the name suggests these birds have been hunted to be served for meals. The birds that fall under the category are pheasants, quails, turkeys, guinea fowl capercaillies, bustards, and rails. The females are quite dull and less colourful than the males.

Pheasants, Quails and Partridges

These birds vary in sizes. They range from small bird and medium to large sized birds. They have more resemblance to chickens. Short, rounded wings, short and thick bill, and stout legs are some of the characteristics of these species of game birds. The pheasants have a longer tail compared to quails and partridges.

Pheasants

Partridges

Turkeys

The turkeys are different from pheasants and thus belong to a different group.

Their heads and necks have close resemblance to those of the guinea fowl. They love open mixed forests as they are woodland birds. They don't fly for long and are not migratory birds.

Turkey

Sea birds

Almost 71per cent of the Earth's surface is covered with water. The oceans are as rich in food as the land, so it is not surprising that birds take advantage of this food supply. Out of bird's 8,700 species only 300 depend on water or sea.

Gull

Shearwater

Albatross

Albatrosses and Shearwaters

Both these birds are great ocean travellers. The shape of their bills gives the name 'tube noses' to their group. The tube is an enlargement of the nostrils of the bird. It enables them to gauge the strength of the air flow or to help them smell food or land.

Some other birds

Another group of sea birds comprises the cormorants, gannets, boobies and frigate. Cormorants are large aquatic birds having long necks and tail, webbed feet and hooked bill.

AMAZING FACT !

* There are in all some 40 species of gulls. They are very successful and adaptable group of birds.
* The wandering Albatross has the broadest wingspan of any living bird, that is up to 3.7 m wide.

Gannet

Boobies

Hunting Birds

Hunting birds are also known as 'birds of prey'. They include eagles, falcons, hawks etc. All of them are gifted with special features that enable them to hunt easily. They have specially designed beaks, feet and bodies. Their eyesight is excellent for catching its prey.

Vultures

Vultures are powerful hunting birds that fall under the category of hunting birds. They usually feed by scavenging. White-backed vulture, the commonest of the vultures, is a disgusting feeder, often entering a carcass to pull out the entrails. Another category of vultures is the king vulture. It is a strange- looking bird that is less found near carcasses. It keeps an eye on its prey and attacks alone. Long- billed and scavenger vultures are the other vultures that are found in the Indian subcontinent. These vultures are commonly found and are good scavengers. They usually hunt in groups unlike the king vultures .

This vulture has huge wings, on which it soarslong distances searching for food. It has a hooked beak which helps it to cut the flesh easily.

Eagles

Eagles are good hunters and can spot their prey from a great height. Eagles are powerful birds and can kill large fishes and other preys. Crested serpent eagle feeds to a large extent on reptiles, frogs and insects. White-eyed buzzard is a dull and sluggish eagle. It likes to spend a lot of time sitting looking-out for a meal. The tawny eagle is found in drier plains of northern and central India.

Eagle

Kites, hawks and owls

Kites, falcons and owls are another group of hunting birds. All these birds are superbly equipped to hunt and kill other animals for food. They have hooked bills and powerful feet with talons. Their sight is better than ours and they have good hearing power. Kites are the most noticeable birds in the subcontinent. Brahmini kites are found by the rivers, lakes or ghouls. Pariah kites boldly swoops down to catch the food. Hawks are the greatest of all hunters. Most owls hunt at night. Their big, forward facing eyes allow them to see in dim light and to judge distance accurately.

owl

Snowy owl hunts during the day as well as at night.

AMAZING FACT !

There is one amazing fact about owls. They sleep all day and hunt for their prey at night. That is why they have round eyes.

Hawk

Ducks, Geese and Swans

Ducks, swans and geese, all are aquatic birds and belong to a family called Anatidae. Ducks are broadly of three types - surface feeding, diving and fish-eating. Swans are long- necked birds and there are eight species of these birds. Geese are swimming birds that migrate in flocks and fly as high as 9,000 m.

Ducks

Ducks are grouped in three groups. Dabbling ducks, such as mallards and shoveller, flit over the surface water in search of food. Diving ducks, like pochard and sawbills, dive below the surface for vegetable matter. Perching ducks, comprising muscovies and the colourful mandarins, nest and perch on trees.

Male ducks usually produce richly coloured feathers each breeding season in order to attract females.

Female ducks, geese and swans of both sexes are plain coloured throughout the year.

Duck

AMAZING FACT !

Geese are smaller than swans but bigger than ducks and spend lesser time in water than either of them.

Ducks feed on seeds, acorns and rice as well as insects.

Geese

This species is found only in the northern hemisphere. They feed on grass and other vegetation.

Grey geese include the greylag goose, which is the ancestor of many farmyard geese. Among the black geese is the Canada goose of North America, which has also been introduced into Britain.

Grey goose

Geese

Swans

Swans have long, flexible necks which enable them to reach plants up to a metre below the surface of the water.

AMAZING FACT !

Swans and geese keep the same mate all their lives but ducks usually find a new mate each season.

Tundra Swans

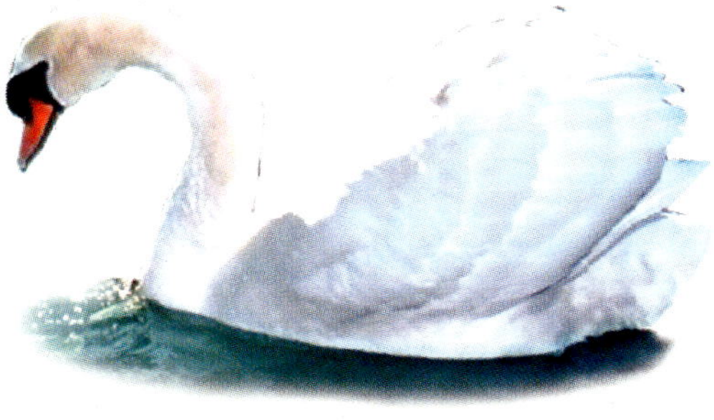

Swan are good swimmers.

Flightless Birds

Flightless birds are the birds with heavy and large bodies and cannot fly because of their weight. This group of birds include the kiwi, emu, ostrich, rhea, penguin and tinamou.

Penguins

Penguins are flightless sea birds that are found in south of the equator, especially in the Antarctic waters. They have a layer of fat deposited under their skin.

Emperor penguin

Penguins like to live in colonies

It acts as a protection amour from the cold. They have streamlined bodies and flipper-like wings that help them shoot along in the water as small torpedoes. They are able to dive because of their heavy bodies.

Ostrich

It is a native of Africa. It is the largest living bird in the world. Its height is around 2.5 metres and can run faster than a horse. It can cover almost 8 metres in one step. Ostriches usually travel in groups.

Ostrich is the largest bird. It can be 25 m high.

Kiwi

Kiwi

Native to New Zealand, the Kiwi is a bird with no tail and wings and rounded back with short, thick legs. Despite having short legs it runs very fast. Its long curved bill is beneficial in pulling out worms from the ground.

Emu

Emu is a huge flightless bird that is a native of Australia. This excellent runner can run at a speed of 45 km per hour. Their basic food is fruits and beans but they are also fond of caterpillars. They mostly love to travel in groups but during breeding they travel in pairs.

Emu

AMAZING FACT !

Ostrich is provided with long powerful legs, with two toes on each foot.

Tinamou

Rhea and tinamou

Rhea and tinamous are flightless birds of Argentina. Rhea is a big and heavy bird that weigh around 25 kg. It is bigger than any other bird of South America. Tinamou is a primitive ground bird with very tiny tail. The tail of some species are so small that they hide it by the body feathers. The body size of female tinamou is larger than that of the male tinamou.

Rhea

Insects 

Together with birds and bats, insects are the only animals that can fly. Insects are numerous in number. Around a million different species have so far been identified, and new ones are being discovered everyday.

Body of an insect

The body of an insect is divided into three main sections. Mouth, eyes and antennae or feelers, which help them smell and feel objects and their enemies, are attached to its head. The legs and the two pair of wings are attached to the next part called thorax. The main part of the gut and the digestive system and sex organs are all in its abdomen.

Group of insects

The insects that are flightless are known as scavengers. Most of the insects have wings and can fly. As young ones they do not have wings but as they grow their wings also start developing and get bigger. When developed completely, they are able to fly. Insects that grow in this manner are said to undergo incomplete metamorphosis. The third category have young that hatch from their eggs as larvae. Most of the insects go through this form of development, termed as complete metamorphosis.

Butterfly undergoes complete metamorphosis.

Dragonfly undergoes incomplete metamorphosis.

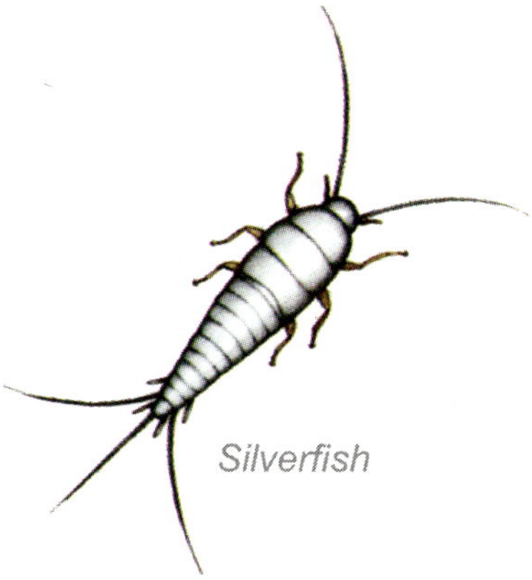

Silverfish

Wingers insects

Some examples of wingless insects are silverfish, bristletail, etc. Silverfish can be found in damp areas of houses, feeding on wallpaper, books clothes or food items.

Insects with incomplete metamorphisms

Termite, book louse, dragonfly and shield bug are some examples of this category of insects. Termite, popularly known as white ant is usually found in warm regions. They feed on wood, paper and vegetation. Dragonfly is an insect with long, slender abdomen, two pairs of transparent wings and big compound eyes. It is a superb flier, some being credited with speeds of 100 mph.

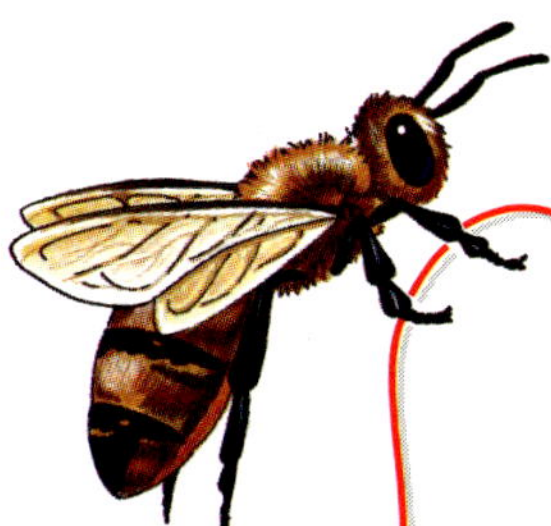

Housefly

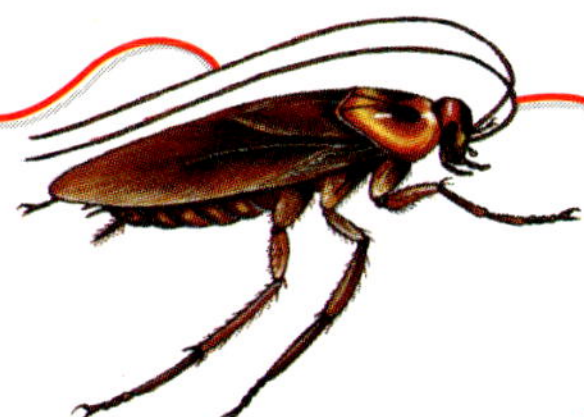

Cockroach

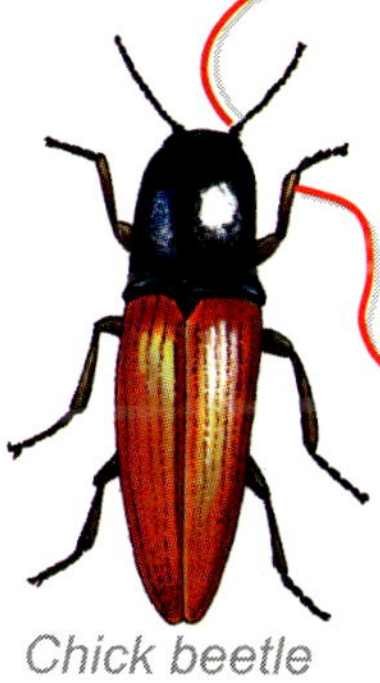

Chick beetle

Fruitfly

Hive of Wasp.

AMAZING FACT !

Dragonflies are the fastest fliers of all insects. Some reach speeds of over 50km in an hour. They are very agile in flight and are able to fly backwards.

Ladybird

Some more Insects 

Scientists think that there are around 7 million kinds of insects that we do not yet know about. The reason for the great numbers of different insects is that they are all small and many of them can share the same environment.

Ants and termites

Ants and termites are insects which always live in groups or colonies. Most ant and termite colonies are large nests. There are thousands of individuals in a colony, but they all have the same mother - the queen.

Termite

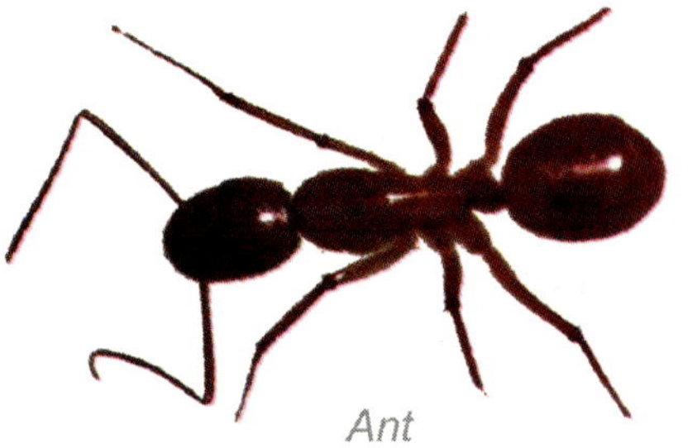

Ant

Fleas and lice

Fleas and lice are wingless insects that live as parasites on other animals. A parasite is an animal that lives by feeding on other animals, usually causing it harm in the process.

AMAZING FACT !

Ants do not have eyes so they follow the trail of the chemical which each of them discharges while moving. This is the reason why they travel in line.

Feather louse

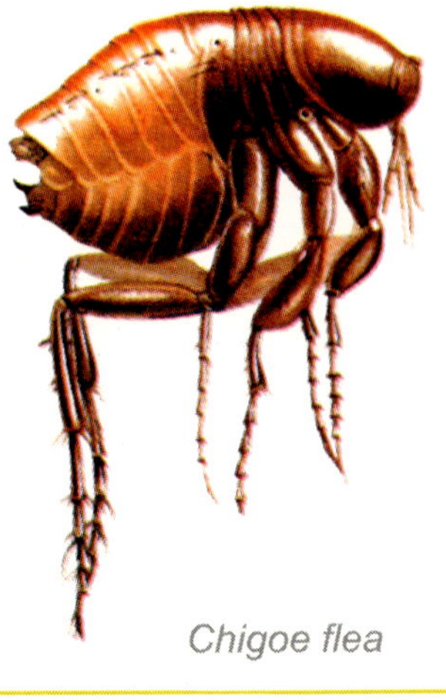

Chigoe flea

Flies and mosquitoes

Flies are among the insects we see most often. They spend the first part of their lives as larvae. Mosquitoes are small flying insects, many of which carry diseases.

Butterfly

Mosquito

Malaria is one of the most serious diseases spread by mosquitoes.

Spiders and scorpions

Spiders and scorpions are related to each other and belong to the group called 'arachnids', which are not insects. Both have the segments of their bodies grouped into two main parts and have eight legs. Both are also hunters, feeding on small prey, which they first poison and then eat.

Scorpion

AMAZING FACT !

When scorpions mate, they perform a special dance, in which the male positions the female over the sperm he has dropped so that she can collect it.

This garden spider is lying in wait for an insect to blunder into its web.

Know About Mammals 

Mammals constitute a very vast and diverse group of animals. They vary from tiny shrews to bulky rhinos, and from whales that spend their entire lives in the oceans to bats that spend the major part of their lives in the air.

Characteristic traits of mammals

All mammals are warm-blooded animals. They, normally, are covered with hair or fur.

The female mammals suckle their young ones with their own supply of milk.

Tigress with its cubs.

Elephant is a mammal.

Mammals have a well defined structure of senses.

The marsupials

Marsupials, such as koalas and kangaroos, are found mainly in Australia and New Guinea. Baby marsupials are tiny when they are born. They depend on their mother's milk to complete their growth. Most of them crawl up their mother's belly to a pouch where they feed on milk and grow in safety.

Koala

Bat

Hippopotamus

The placentals

Most mammals including whales, bats, giraffes, hippopotamuses and human beings, are placentals. Young placentals grow inside their mother's body for a long time before they are born. They are nourished through a special organ called the placenta which develops within the mother's body.

Giraffe is the tallest land animal. It feeds on leaves upto 6 metre above the ground.

AMAZING FACT !

Mammals Record
Largest: Blue whale, up to 33m in length and about 120 tonnes in weight.
Smallest: Several kinds of shrew have a head and body length of less than 4.5 cm and weigh about 2g.

Shrew is the smallest animal in the world. Its body length is less than 4.5 cm.

The Dog and Cat Family

There are more than 100 different breeds of domestic dogs that live and work with people all over the world. But there are many other kinds of wild dogs as well, including wolves, foxes, jackals and coyotes. The cat family includes wild cats such as lions, tigers, leopards and cheetahs, and domestic cats.

Bull dog

Mastiff

Fox terrier

Alsatian

Wild and domestic dogs

Wolves live in family groups called packs. The pack centres around a breeding pair who mate for life and can contain up to 20 members. Because wolves hunt together, they can kill animals that are much larger than themselves.

They eat a wide variety of foods, such as small rodents, insects, and even woodland fruits.

Dogs were the first animals to be domesticated and they are now found wherever there are human beings.

Cat family

The cat family comprise lions, tigers, leopards, cheetahs and jaguars. They are known as big cats. Domestic cats are the ones that we keep as pets in our homes. Unlike most members of the cat family, lions live in groups called prides. A pride usually consists of about a dozen animals. Tigers are big cats that live in forested areas. They are good swimmers and can climb quite well. Leopards usually live alone and defend their territories from others. They climb trees very well and often rest up in the branches. They mainly hunt medium-sized grazing animals such as small antelopes and pigs.

Tiger

Lion

Cat

AMAZING FACT !

Cats are popular pets. They were first tamed by the ancient Egyptians at least 3,500 years ago.

Horse Family

For thousands of years, and in almost all parts of the world, people have used horses for riding, to pull heavy loads and for sports and leisure. Herds of wild horses still survive in some parts of the world, but the zebras of Africa are very rare.

Know about horses

Wild horses live in herds in open grassland, in Africa, the Middle East and Asia. They have sharp sense of sight, hearing and smell, and can detect hunting animals from a distance. They are strong runners, and use their speed over long distances to escape from danger.

Horses are the most expensive domestic animals.

Domestication of horses

At first, they were used to pull lightweight chariots, but when larger breeds were developed, people began to ride. With the arrival of the horse collar, people began to use horses to pull heavy weights.

During the Middle Ages, the armour worn by knights was so heavy that only very big horses could carry their weight. Huge animals, called the great horses, were bred. More lightweight, speedier horses were bred in countries surrounding the Mediterranean Sea. These were the ancestors of the fast, slender-limbed horses such as the Arab breeds.

Horses were first domesticated by prehistoric people in Central Asia.

AMAZING FACT !

A pony is a small horse, standing less than 142 cm at the withers (the high-point between its shoulder-blades).

Zebra

Zebra is a stocky African wild horse with bold black and white stripes. Three species of zebras are known: *Equus grevyi,* with narrow stripes; *Equus zebra* (mountain zebra), with loose flap of skin on throat, and short crosswise stripes on top of hindquarter; and *Equus burchelli,* the common zebra.

Zebra is a striped animal that belongs to the horse family.

Sheep and goats 

Sheep and goats are naturally agile, sturdily built animals, related to cattle. They are now rare in the wild, but many domestic varieties have been bred from the wild species.

Sheep

Sheep

Most wild sheep and goats live in mountainous areas.

Sheep are good climbers but less agile than goats, so they are generally found at lower and less rocky levels. Sheep and goats both have horns, which are larger in the males. They are used particularly in fighting for mates.

In the wintertime wild sheep grow a thick undercoat (fleece) of fine wool to keep them warm and dry. It is moulted (shed) completely in the summer. People started keeping sheep so that this fleece could be shorn off each year and used to make wool.

Sheep fleece is used to make wool.

There are now more than 800 breeds and over 800 million domestic sheep.

Male sheep are known as Ram.

Gazelle

The gazelle is an elegant athletic antelope, native to Africa and South Asia. It is usually pale brown from the top with white underparts; some species have thick black line along side; face often has weak stripes. When gazelles are alarmed, they move by 'pronking' (or 'stotting') - a vertical leap using all four legs simultaneously.

Gazelle

AMAZING FACT !

Sheep and goats are ruminants, like cattle and antelopes. This means they eat plants and then regurgitate the food to chew it again.

Goat

The goat is a mammal of Bovidae family; and is classified as an antelope. It has a tail with naked undersurface. Both sexes have horns but only males have beard. Goats inhabit dry rugged country; browse on coarse vegetation. Male goat is called a billy, female a nanny, and young a kid.

Wild goats live in herds. They have coats made of thick, often coarse hair. Many varieties of goats have been domesticated and have been kept for their milk, meat and skins.

Mountain Goat

Cattle and Camels

Cattle include a number of large plant-eating animals such as cows, buffaloes and bison. A few kinds of cattle are still found in the wild, but most live as farm animals and are a vital source of milk, meat and leather.

Kinds of cattle

There are several different kinds of wild cattle, including yaks, bison and buffaloes. Many live in forested areas where they can find plenty of food and safe, shady places to rest. However, some, such as yaks, live in high mountain areas of the Himalayas.

Yak

Others, such as the American bison, live on vast plains where they graze on the plentiful grass.

Cattle are social animals and live in groups led by a bull. Both males and females have horns. They are straight or curved and last all through the animal's life.

The horns of water buffalo are bigger than those of any other animal.

Oxen are used to carry loads. They assist in farming.

Domestic cattle

Today there are about 200 different domestic breeds. They are mostly bred for their milk, meat and leather. However, some are also used for pulling ploughs and heavy loads. Cattle droppings can be used as fertilizer, and sometimes they are dried out and used as fuel to light fires.

Cows

Buffalo

Camels

Camels are the largest animals of the desert. Thcy are well suited to the harsh, waterless environment. Camels' bodies are adapted to save water in the dry desert. They do not sweat, and they lose very little moisture in other ways.

Camel can go without drinking for long periods, losing up to 40 per cent of its body weight. A camel's two-toed, broad-padded feet are ideal for walking on loose sand or gravel, and it can close its nostrils against sandstorms.

AMAZING FACT !

Camels' humps do not contain water, it is actually the fat which is used up when water is not available.

Camel is known as "The Ship of Desert."

Elephants 

Elephants are the biggest living land animals. There are two kinds of elephant : one lives in Africa, the other in Asia. African elephants are rarely tamed, but Asiatic ones are often used to move heavy objects such as logs, and for ceremonial processions.

Difference between Asiatic and African elephants

Asiatic elephants measure up to 6.4 m in length and weigh up to 5000 kg. They have triangular ears and rounded back with two bulges on forehead. Their tusks are small and the females have no tusks at all.

African elephants grow in length up to 7.5 m and weigh up to 7,500 kg. They have large, rounded ears and hollowed back. Their foreheads are rounded and they have large tusks.

Trunks, tusks and teeth

An elephant's trunk is formed from its upper lip and nose. The elephant uses it to smell, breathe and drink. The trunk is also used as a hand.

An elephant's tusks are really just big teeth.

African elephants

Elephants use their tusks for defence and in feeding. An adult elephant eats about 150 kg of grass, leaves, twigs and fruit each day. Elephants have grinding teeth in the back of their mouths.

Elephants in danger

Present-day elephants are endangered because humans are increasingly taking over the land where they live and also killing them for their valuable ivory tusks. Ivory has always been much prized for carving and making luxury items.

AMAZING FACT !

An elephant's skull is large but comparatively light in weight. It has two front teeth (incisors) which form the tusks. Its back teeth (molars) are replaced as they wear out.

An elephant has two front teeth which form the tusks.

Whales and Seals 

Whales may look like fishes, with smooth, streamlined bodies perfectly adapted for life in water, but in fact they are mammals - just like us. They are very intelligent animals, and they produce a single live young, which they feed on milk.

Whales

There are two main types of whale. The toothed whales include the smaller dolphins and porpoises, as well as giants such as the sperm whale. These animals use their pointed teeth to catch and hold fish or squid.

The baleen whales are all large and include the right whale and the enormous blue whale. These whales feed on shrimp-like creatures called krill, which they sift out of the water with huge fringed plates in their mouths.

Whales can hear very well (even though they have no visible ears). Some use sounds we call whale songs to communicate with each other.

Whale

Blue Whale

Seals

Seals and their relatives, the sea lions and walruses, are sea mammals. Although they spend most of their lives in the water, they breathe air.

Seals can stay in the water for long periods. Beneath their skin, they have a thick coat of special fat called blubber, which helps to keep them warm.

Grey seals use their long whiskers to detect changes in water pressure as something swims past, so they can catch prey even in murky water.

Dolphins

Dolphins are small, slender whales, some of which are capable of swimming at speeds of about 50 kilometres per hour. Most of them have a large, curved fin in the middle of the back that helps to stabilize them.

Many kinds of dolphins have a long snout crammed with up to 200 small pointed teeth, ideal for catching fish. The largest of the dolphins, the killer whales, sometimes hunt in packs to catch much bigger animals.

AMAZING FACT !

Dolphins are thought to be among the most intelligent of animals. They are sometimes kept and trained to do tricks and to help underwater engineers.

Dolphin

Bulky Animals

Bears, hippos and rhinos are huge and bulky animals that weigh more than three times as much as a lion. They are found in a wide range of habitats. Rhinos are different from other mammals as they have horns on top of their heads.

Bears

Bears are large animals that are found in places ranging from the Arctic areas to tropical forests. The bears found in the Arctic region are called polar bears. Polar bears feed mainly on fish and seals but other bears generally have a varied diet, that includes fruits, honey, nuts, and small animals.

Like human beings, bears can stand upright. They have poor eyesight and hearing, but their sense of smell is excellent. They generally live alone. In the autumn, when food is abundant, bears eat a lot. They do not go into a deep hibernation (winter sleep) and are usually able to wake up quickly.

Sloth bear

Grizzly bear

Hippopotamus

Hippos

Hippopotamus is one of the largest living terrestrial mammals distantly related to the pig, wide-spread in Africa. Hippopotamuses generally are about 1.6m tall and weigh about 4,500 kg. They have massive bodies set on short legs, each with four toes and hoof-like nails. They spend most of the day submerged in rivers.

AMAZING FACT !

White rhinos are in fact grey-white in colour. The 'white' in their name comes from an Afrikaans word meaning 'wide' and refers to their broad lips.

Rhinos

Rhinoceroses, or rhinos, are large horned mammals that live in the tropical grasslands and forests of Africa and Asia. All five surviving kinds of rhinoceroses are in danger of becoming extinct.

A white rhino with its calf. White rhinos are in fact grey-brown in colour.

Apes and their Family

Apes are our nearest relatives in the animal kingdom. Like humans, they are intelligent, long-lived mammals, and they generally travel in family parties. There are two main groups of apes. Gorillas, chimapanzees and orang-utans are the great apes, and gibbons and siamangs are the lesser apes.

Characteristics of apes

The great apes have bodies much like ours. Like us, they have 32 teeth. Female apes, like humans, normally have one baby at a time. Young apes develop slowly. Apes mainly eat leaves and fruit, though some also feed on flesh, and insects. They wakeup early and roam through the forest in search of food.

During the middle of the day they doze in nests of branches and leaves, which they build in the trees.

Mandril

Chimpanzee

Orang-utans are the large sized apes.

Gorillas are the largest of the apes, growing up to 1.75 m.

Proboscis monkey

Category of apes

Chimpanzees live in the forests of central and western Africa. They use gestures and facial expressions to give information to other members of the group. Gorillas are the largest of the great apes. They live in the forests of Central Africa. Gorillas are unaggressive creatures, and live in family groups led by a big male. The word 'orang-utan' means 'man of the woods'. Orangs live in forests on the islands of Sumatra and Borneo in South-east Asia. Unlike the other great apes, they mostly live alone.

AMAZING FACT !

Like humans, apes are primates. This means that their hands have a thumb which can be pressed against a finger to pick things up, although they cannot fold it across the palm of the hand.

Unit-5

The World of Plants

Plant Characteristics

Plants are the green-coloured organisms that are able to make their own food by the process of photosynthesis. Plants range in size from giant trees to tiny mosses. They include the largest and the oldest living things. But unlike animals, they grow rooted in the soil or attached to the ground or to rocks.

How do plants develop ?

Plants do not feed like animals, although they have to take in chemicals from the soil or from their surroundings to grow. Instead of eating, most make their own food in special 'chemical factories' in their leaves. The plants form the first links in the food chain.

Plants make their own food in the leaves.

Photosynthesis

Plants make their food by a process known as photosynthesis. It requires sunlight, water and carbon dioxide. Photosynthesis is carried out mostly in the leaves, where the pigment that gives leaves their green colour, called chlorophyll, is stored. Oxygen is released during this process.

Sunlight supplies energy for the process

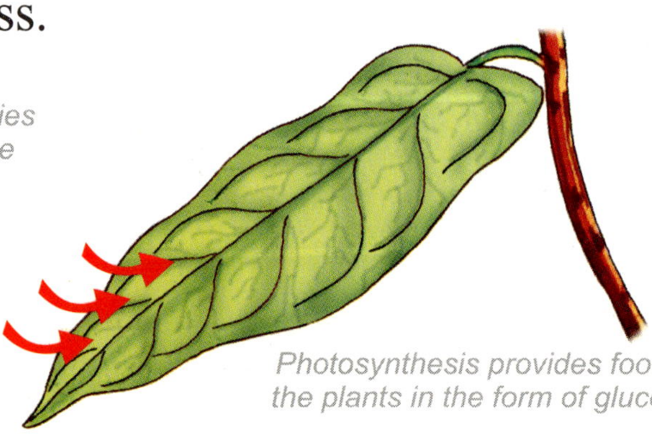

Photosynthesis provides food to the plants in the form of glucose.

Food stores

The sugars produced by plants in photosynthesis can be joined together and stored as more complex chemicals called starches. The plant can break down the starch and the sugars whenever it needs energy, for example, at night when there is no sunlight to provide energy, or when it needs extra energy to grow or to produce seeds.

Petunia

Flowers

Flowers enable a plant to be pollinated and then to form seeds. Flowers consist of male and female organs surrounded by petals that may be coloured and scented to attract visiting animals.

AMAZING FACT !

Some plants living in acid, boggy soils make food by photosynthesis but get some nutrients from animals. The Venus Fly Trap has a spring-trap mechanism that allows it to catch insects.

Hibiscus

The male parts of a flower make pollen and the female parts make cells that form seeds.

Sunflower

Rose

Flowers constitute the reproductive parts of a plant.

Fungi

Fungi are an important group of living things. They get their food by breaking down the tissues of living or dead plants or animals. Many fungi can only be seen with a microscope. A few, such as mushrooms and toadstools, grow much larger.

How do they grow?

Most fungi grow as networks of tiny threads known as *hyphae*. These spread through the material on which the fungus is growing, and absorb food. Fungi reproduce by way of microscopic spores, which act like tiny seeds. They are produced in a part of the fungus called the fruiting body.

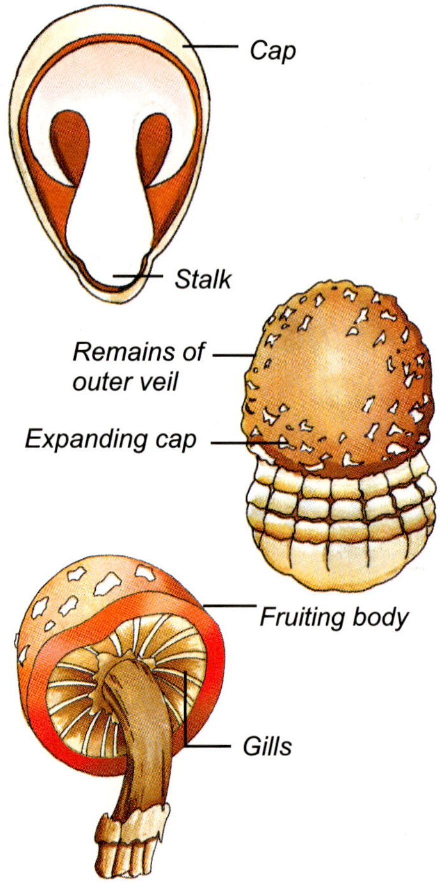

In fungi, the spores help in reproduction.

Toadstools

Mushrooms

Toadstools and mushrooms

Toadstools and mushrooms are the fruiting bodies of some kinds of fungus. They are usually umbrella-shaped, with a thick stalk and a broad cap. Beneath the cap there are hanging curtains called gills or pores, where the spores develop. Many kinds of mushrooms are edible, but only two are grown widely for food.

Useful fungi

One vital role of fungi is to decompose dead plants, animals and their wastes. Fungi break the dead matter down into chemicals that are recycled back into the soil. Other fungi are essential partners in the growth of trees and other plants. They live in or around their roots in a mass called a mycorrhiza. The roots protect the fungi, which in turn provide food for the plants. Yeasts are another type of fungus that are used in making bread, beer and wine. Other fungi produce penicillin and other antibiotics, which attack bacteria harmful to humans.

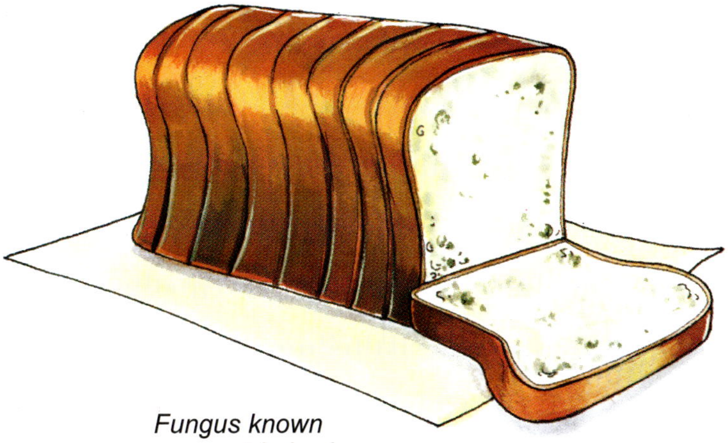

Fungus known as yeast helps in rising of bread.

AMAZING FACT !

Some fungi grow so fast that a single spore can produce more than 1 km of hyphae in 24 hours.

Wine and beer are made using the fungus yeast.

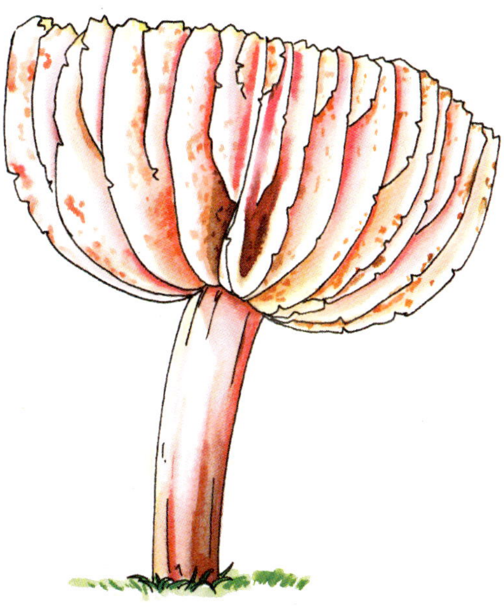

Fruiting body of a fungus.

Plant Cells and Tissues

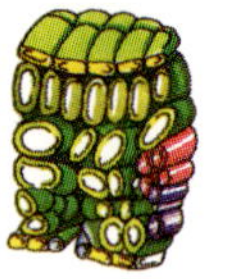

Every living thing is made up of tiny structures called cells. A plant has a number of different types of cells, each one plays an important part in keeping it alive, such as absorbing water and minerals for making food.

Plant tissue

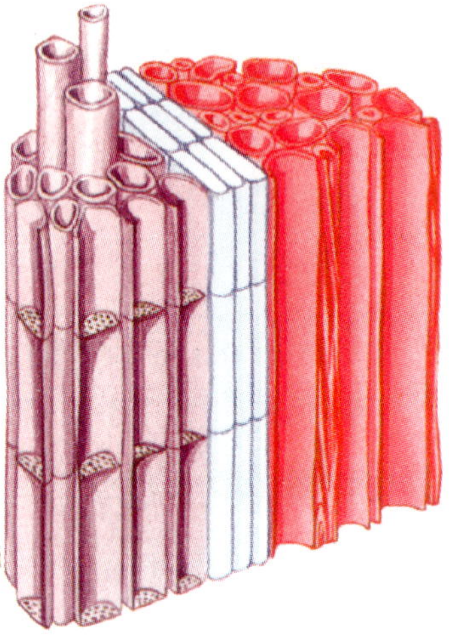

Cross section of vascular tissue.

Almost every plant, except for algae, mosses and liverworts, are called vascular plants. This means that they have a complex system of vascular tissue, which gives support and carries food and water through the plant. Vascular tissue is made-up of two main kinds of tissue, known as xylem and phloem. Water is taken up from the roots by xylem. In flowering plants, this is made-up of tubes called vessels. These have long, thin cells called fibres providing support between them. Food manufactured in the leaves, dissolves in water and is carried to all parts of the plant by phloem. This is the made-up of fluid-carrying cells called sieve tubes. The initial tissue formed by a new plant is called primary tissue.

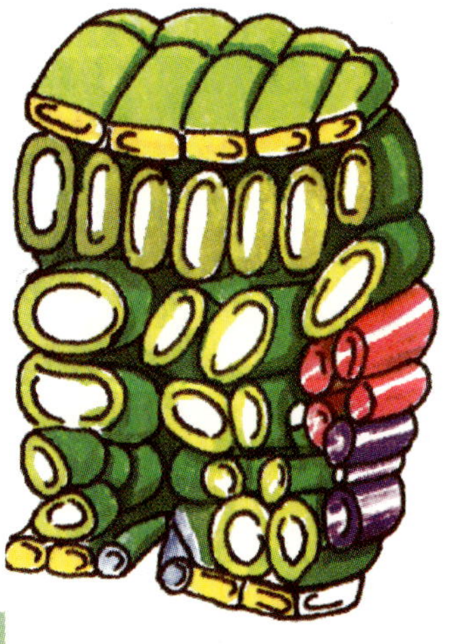

Cross section of a plant cell.

Cell structure

Plant cells are similar to animal cells in many ways, but they are generally larger and have some features which are not found in animal cells. Most of these help the plant to make its own food, inside its cells. Around each plant cell is a cell wall. Directly beneath the cell wall there is a thin layer called the cell membrane.

Inside a stem

In new stems, vascular tissue is usually arranged in groups known as vascular bundles. These are surrounded by a tissue called cortex. In plants called dicotyledons, the bundles are arranged in a regular pattern. In older dicotyledon stems, the bundles join up to form a central core known as the vascular cylinder.

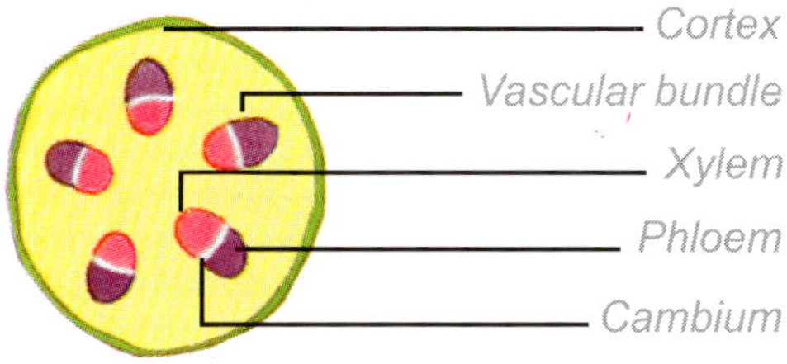

Cross section of a new dicotyledon stem

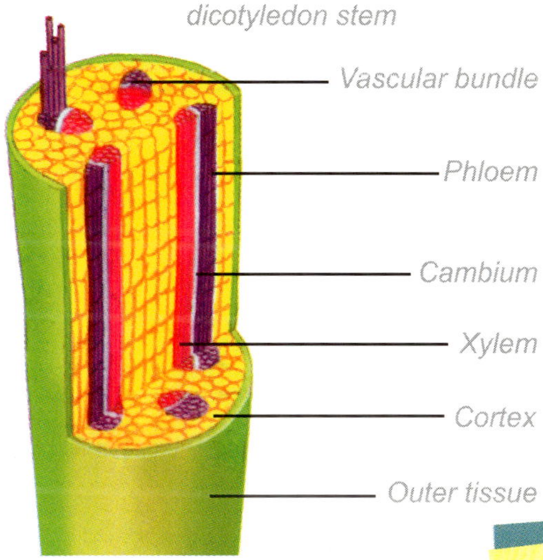

Cutaway of a young dicotyledon stem

Inside a root

In a new root, the tissue is arranged in a different manner from a stem. A central core forms as the plant gets mature.

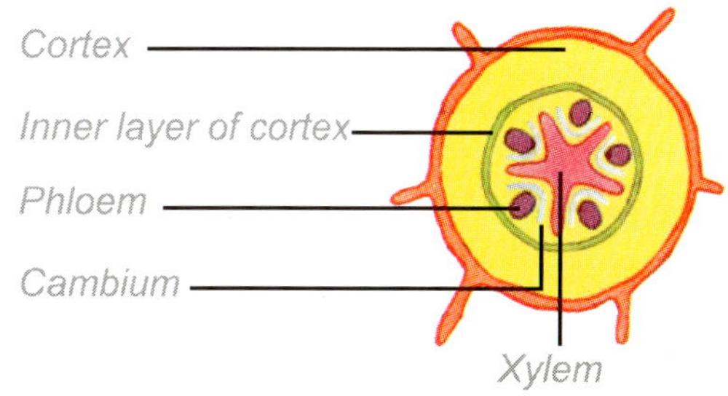

Cross section of a young dicotyledon root

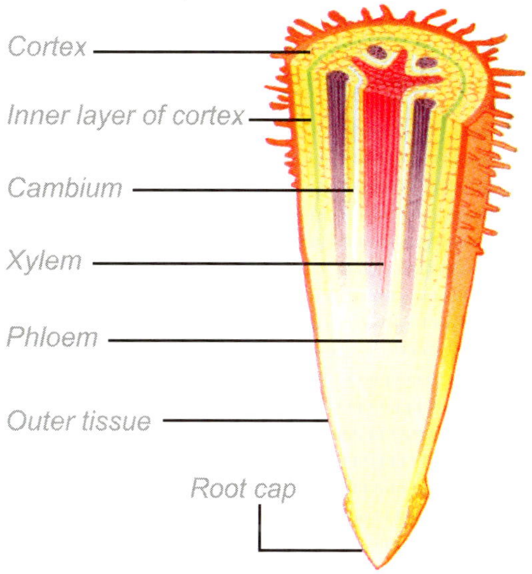

Cutaway of a young dicotyledon root

AMAZING FACT!

Non-vascular plants are widely believed to have evolved from complex green algae that grew on land more than 400 million years ago.

Stems and Roots

A plant is mainly supported by its stem and roots. In most plants, these also play an important part in carrying fluids. The stem and roots are made-up of various parts, which change as the plant gets older.

Stem and roots

The stem is the major above-ground or aerial part of a plant. It supports the plant, usually growing upwards. Stems contain a system of vascular tissue, which carries water and minerals throughout the plant. A shoot is a new stem which grows out of a seed or off the main stem of a plant. A bud is a small growth on a stem, which develops into either a new shoot or a flower. There are two different kinds of buds, called terminal and auxillary buds. Auxillary buds are also known as lateral or secondary buds.

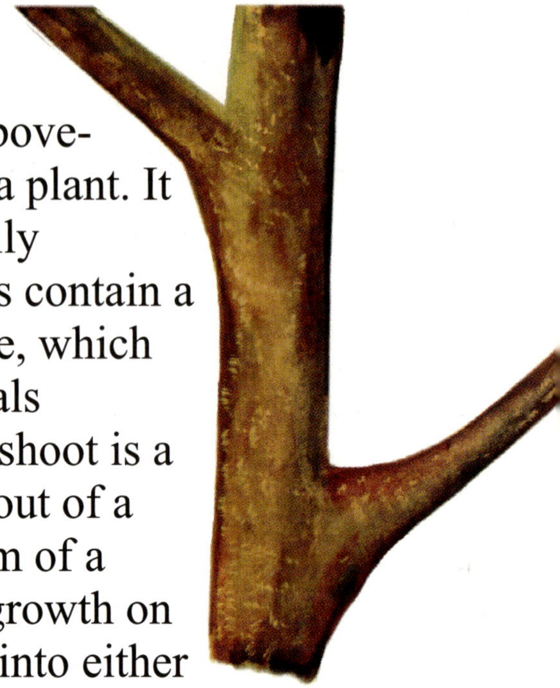

This thick stem contains a system of tubes, which carry water and food through the plant.

Growth

A group of cells which divide to provide new growth is called a meristem. The main meristems are at the tip of the shoot and root. They are called apical meristems. A meristem formed in the main stem or a shoot is a part of a terminal bud.

Meristems are found here.

AMAZING FACT!

The giant bamboo of Myanmar (Burma) grows at up to 46 cm a day, making it one of the fastest growing of all plants.

Parts of a root

The root of a plant usually grows down into the ground. Its main purpose is to take in water and minerals from the soil. These are absorbed through tiny, thread-like structures called root hairs. The root also acts as an anchor, holding the plant firmly in the soil.

A root grows when cells just behind its tip divide. The new cells have soft cell walls which allow them to stretch lengthwise as water is taken into the root.

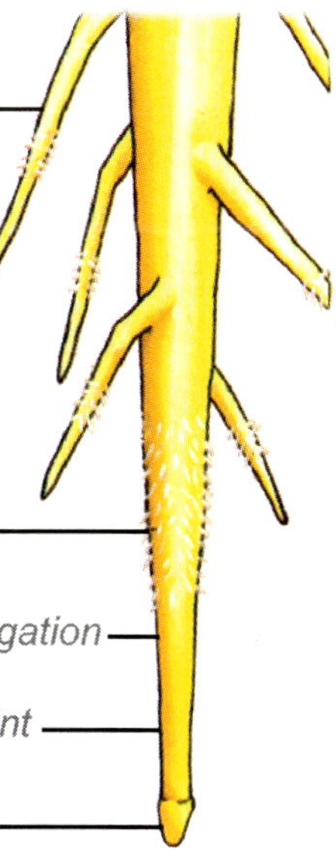

Types of roots

A 'tap root' is a large root with smaller ones growing out of it. These small roots are called lateral roots. Many vegetables, such as carrots, are swollen tap roots and are known as root vegetables.

'Fibrous roots' are a system of many equal-sized roots, all of which produce smaller lateral roots.

Adventitious roots grow directly from a stem.

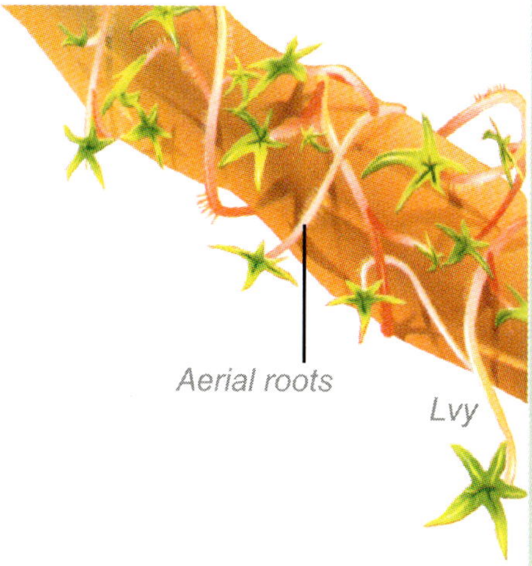

'Aerial roots' do not normally grow in the ground. Many can absorb moisture from the air.

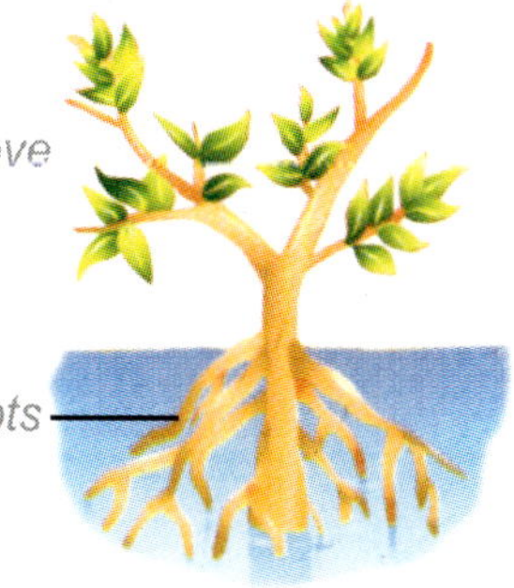

'Prop root' is a particular kind of aerial root that grows outwards from a stem, then down into the ground.

Leaves, Flowers and Fruits

The leaves of a green plant are its main food-making parts. They make food by a process called photosynthesis. A plant's leaves are collectively called its foliage. There are many different sizes and shapes of leaves, but only two main types: simple and compound leaves. There are over 250,000 different kinds of flowering plants.

Simple leaves

Simple leaves are made up of a single leaf blade, called a lamina. Lilies, elms and maples are examples of plants with simple leaves.

Some leaves are green due to the presence of chlorophyll and some are not due to the absence of chlorophyll.

Compound leaves

Compound leaves are made-up of small leaf blades called leaflets, which grow from a central leaf stalk. Clovers and ferns are examples of plants with compound leaves. The number and arrangement of leaflets on a compound leaf vary from plant to plant.

AMAZING FACT!

Fruit life can be extended by both refrigeration and controlled atmosphere.

Blue Bell

Dahlia

Rose

Hibiscus

Tiger Lily

Flowers

Most of the plants around us have flowers at some time. The flowers contain the plants' reproductive organs which produce seeds. A typical flower has a number of sepals around the outside. They protect the flower bud and may fall off when the bud opens. The most obvious parts of the flower are the petals. These are often brightly coloured and they attract insects to the flower for pollination.

Types of fruits

Fruit protect the seeds they carry and help them to scatter to a place where they can grow. Many fruits grow from a plant's ovary. These are termed as true fruit. Some like strawberries, grow from the receptacle and the ovary. They are false fruit.

Some common fruits

Dry fruits

Dry fruits are dry cases that hold the seeds until they are ripe. There are many types. The main ones are: nuts, achenes, grains.

Some common dry fruits.

Plant Senses

Every living creature can respond to changes in their surroundings. This is termed as sensitivity to a stimulus. Plants do not have a specialized nervous system, but they are still able to react to stimuli like temperature, touch and light.

Plant response

Many plants react to a stimulus by a source approaching towards or getting away from it. This reaction is known as tropism. Approaching towards stimulus is called positive tropism, and getting away from it is called negative tropism.

Tropisms are controlled by auxins. These are growth hormones made in the plant's cells.

Vines have tendriils that twine around a support.

Plant going towards light

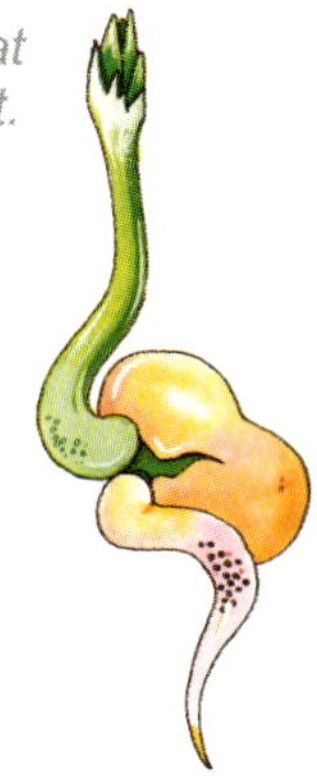

Plant responding to gravity.

Reacting to touch

Few plants are sensitive to touch. This reaction, which is defined as haptotropism or thigmotropism, can help a plant in different ways. For example, flesh-eating plants trap their food when it touches sensitive parts on their surface.

In some plants, touch causes a response which acts as a defence. For example, the leaves of touch-me-not instantly close whenever touched. Touch causes the pressure of water in its leaf cells to drop.

The tendrils of this sweet peas's plant help it to climb.

Open leaf

Closed leaf

Touch-me-not

Responding to light

Almost every plant responds to the amount of light available and the direction from which it is coming. This reaction is termed as phototropism. For example, the leaves of many plants turn to face the Sun. This enables them to absorb light for photosynthesis.

Chrysanthemums flowers when the nights are long.

Larkspur flower when the nights are short.

Snapdragon flowers in both the conditions.

AMAZING FACT !

Some plants feed on animals! When a fly settles between its jaw-like leaves, the Venus fly trap snaps shut and the unfortunate fly is slowly digested.

Sunflower

The sunflower responds to light by turning to face the Sun.

You must have noticed a sunflower facing towards the sunlight. A sunflower usually faces the sun and turns according to the direction of the sun.

Living Style of Plants 

The way a plant grows and reproduces depends on many things, such as climate, soil and weather conditions. Some plants grow quickly and reproduce many times when conditions are right. Others may grow one year and reproduce the next.

Annuals

Flowering plants that live and die within a single year are called annuals. The entire process of growth, flowering and seed production may take place in as little as a few weeks. Annual plants usually bloom and die by the end of the summer.

Lobelia flower grows, flowers and dies within a year.

Biennials grow and store food in one year, then flower and die in the next.

Biennials

Some flowering plants take two years to complete their life cycle. They are called biennials. During the first year, they grow and store up food. In the second year, the plant grows taller, blooms and produces seeds. After this, the entire plant dies.

Perennials

Plants that live for many years are called perennials. There are two types. Herbaceous perennials lose all the parts that are above ground each winter. Shrubs and trees are woody perennials. They may lose some parts, such as leaves, during the winter, but their stems or trunks stay alive, growing thicker each year.

Trees are woody perennials that live for many years.

AMAZING FACT !

Flowers open at different times of the day. The geranium opens in the morning, the marvel-of Peru in the evening.

Desert flowers bloom during the brief rainy season.

Ephemerals

Plants with very short life cycles are called ephemeral plants. They are often found where the right growth conditions occur for a limited time, such as in deserts. The plants grow quickly from seeds which have been inactive in the ground. They bloom and produce seeds, which may also then grow, bloom and produce seeds, and so on, until conditions become unsuitable again.

Plant Food

Unlike animals, most plants can make the food that they need. These plants are described as autotrophic. A small number of plants do photosynthesis, but feed on living things.

Photosynthesis

Photosynthesis uses water sunlight, and carbon dioxide from the air. It takes place mainly in a plant's leaves, in the long, column-shaped palisade cells. Palisade cells contain tiny structures called chloroplasts. Chloroplasts contain a green chemical called chlorophyll which absorbs the Sun's light energy. This is used to power photosynthesis. Carbon dioxide from the air is taken in through the surface of the leaves, and the roots take in water from the soil. This process produces chemicals called carbohydrates and also oxygen. Most of the food is used to produce energy for growth. The food that is not needed straight away is stored in the cells as a substance called starch.

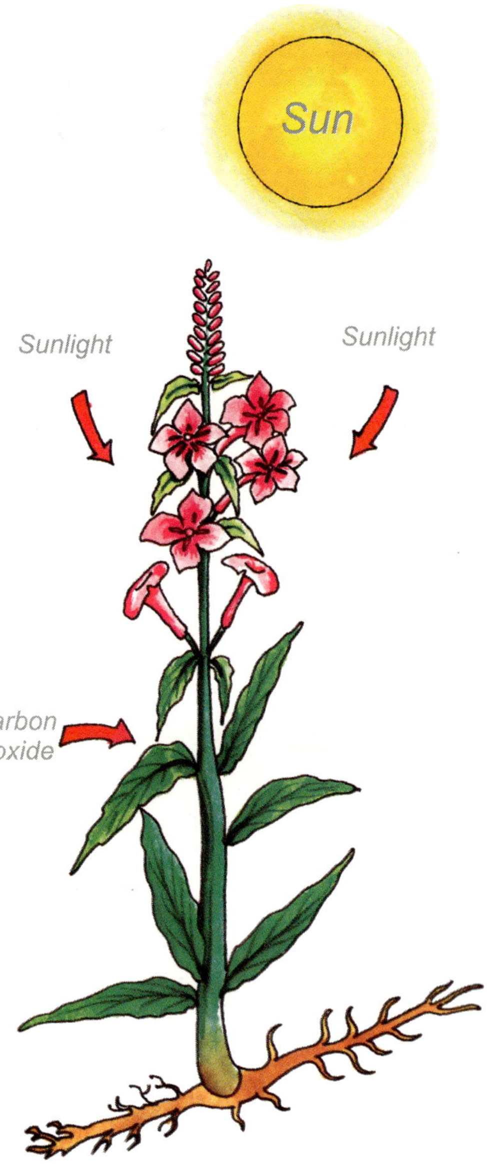

Nitrates and other minerals taken in by the roots are used to build new tissue.

AMAZING FACT !

Trees release a lot of the oxygen we need to breathe and stay alive. So forests are often described as the lungs of the Earth.

Compensation points

At dusk and dawn, the process of photosynthesis and respiration are equally balanced. This means that photosynthesis produces just the correct amount of carbohydrates and oxygen for respiration, produces the correct amount of carbon dioxide and water for photosynthesis. These are termed as compensation points.

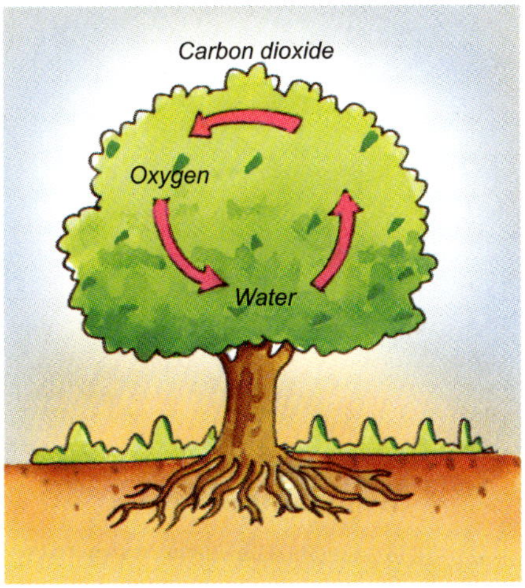

At dawn, rates of photosynthesis and respiration are equal.

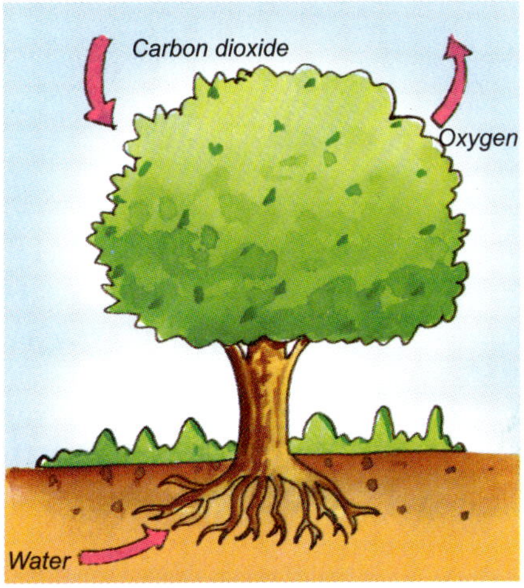

During the day the light is bright, so photosynthesis is faster.

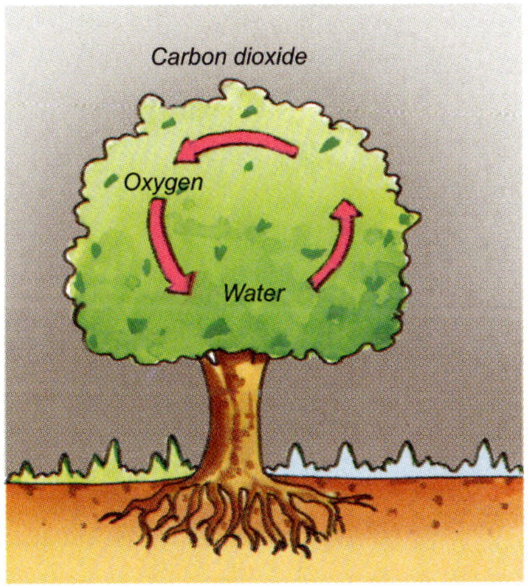

At dusk, rates of photosynthesis and respiration are equal.

At night there is no sunlight, so no photosynthesis takes place.

Working together

The process of photosynthesis and internal respiration are linked closely. During the day, photosynthesis produces oxygen and carbohydrates, which are both required for respiration. At night respiration produces carbon dioxide and water, which are required for photosynthesis.

Classification of Plants

To make living things easier to study, scientists classify them into various groups with similar qualities. This process is termed as classification. Usually plants are classified by comparing the structure of their stems and leaves, as well as the arrangement and types of their reproductive parts.

The kingdoms of life

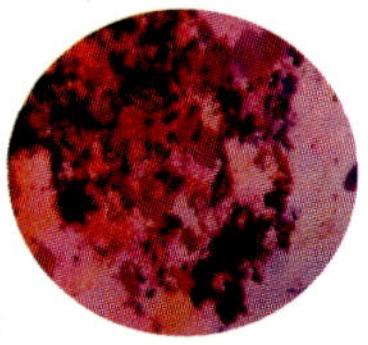
Bacteria

The largest groups into which scientists divide living things are termed as kingdoms. There are five major kingdom:

Amoeba

Monera

Simple microscopic organisms, such as bacteria, which do not have a nucleus in their cells.

Diatom

Protista

Single-celled organisms, such as amoebas, which share features with both plants and animals.

Plants

Living things such as trees and grass, which contain chlorophyll. Most of them make their own food by photosynthesis, but a small number digest other living things.

Flower

Fungus

Fungi

Plant-like organisms that lack chlorophyll, and therefore cannot photosynthesize. Some of them break down dead matter, while others feed on living things.

Animals

Creatures that can usually move around, and eat plants or other animals for food. Mammals and insects are examples of animals.

Zebra

AMAZING FACT !

Plants can also catch diseases. In general, a plant becomes diseased when it suffers from nutrient deficiency or is infected by a virus.

Summary of divisions in the plant kingdom

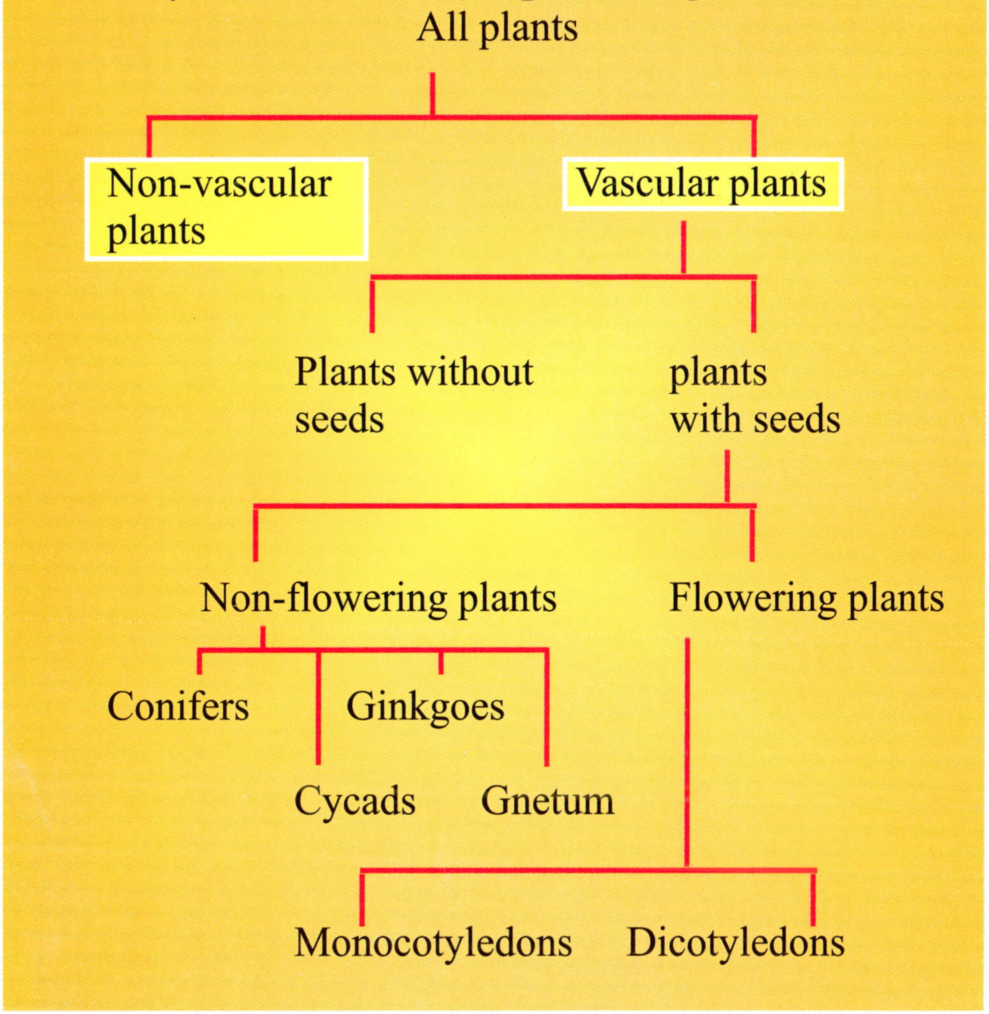

AMAZING FACT !

The earliest evidence for land plants consists of isolated spores, tracheid-like tubes, and sheets of cells found in Ordovician rocks.

Flowering and Non-Flowering Plants

There are over 250,000 different kinds of flowering plants. Plants which produce flowers are known as Anthophytes. Liverworts, mosses, ferns, algae and horsetails are known as flowerless plants.

Flowers

Flowers contain the parts of plants needed for reproduction. These produce male and female sex cells, called gametes, which join together to create new plants of the same kind. Flowers are made-up of many specialized parts. These include petals, stamens (the male parts), and one or more carpels (the female parts). In most plants, the petals are arranged in a circle, around the male and female parts.

Rose is a flowering plant. Roses are very beautiful flowers that come in various colours.

Just before a plant blooms, it produces a bud, which will eventually develop into a flower. It grows from the expanded tip of a stalk, called the receptacle. Buds are surrounded and protected by small, leaf-like sepals.

Liverworts

Liverworts are low-growing plants that live in damp places on soil on rocks. They do not have true roots, stems or leaves. The main part of a liverwort is called the thallus. It is held in the ground by simple root-like growths called rhizoids.

Liverworts

Mosses

Mosses

Mosses are low-growing plants that live in damp, shady places, for example, on walls, rocks and tree trunks. They absorb large amounts of water through their many tiny leaf-like structure, which are only one cell thick.

Ferns

There are over 10,000 species of ferns. They grow in damp, shady places all over the world. Unlike mosses and liverworts, they have true leaves, stems and roots, with well-developed vascular tissue. This helps them to survive in drier conditions, and also to grow taller to get a better share of the light.

Ferns

AMAZING FACT !

The largest flowers in the world belong to the rafflesia. A flower can be one metre wide and weigh almost seven kg.

Vascular and Non-Vascular Plants

Plants are organised in large groups known as divisions. The plant kingdom has two major divisions: Plants which consist of fluid-carrying vascular tissue, and plants which do not. These positions then break down into further, smaller categories, based mainly on the plants reproductive structures.

Vascular Plants

Vascular plants are grouped into two categories: those which germinate seeds, and those which do not. Plants that germinate seeds can be categorized into two further groups, the gymnophytes and the anthophytes.

Gymnophytes

The seeds are not contained within a fruit. There are four types of gymnophytes.

Cycad

Anthophytes

Anthophytes is the name given to the many thousands of different flowering plants. They all produce seeds which are enclosed within a fruit of some kind. Flowering plants can be divided into two further groups: monocotyledons and dicotyledons.

AMAZING FACT !

Plants can also catch diseases. In general, a plant becomes diseased when it is continuously disturbed by some causal agent that results in an abnormal physiological process.

Ferns

Non-Vascular Plants

Plants without vascular tissue, called mosses and liverworts, as bryophytes. They are usually small, with single-celled root-like structures, and simple leaves. They have no flowers and therefore reproduce using spores. Most develop in damp, shady places.

Summary of divisions in the plant kingdom

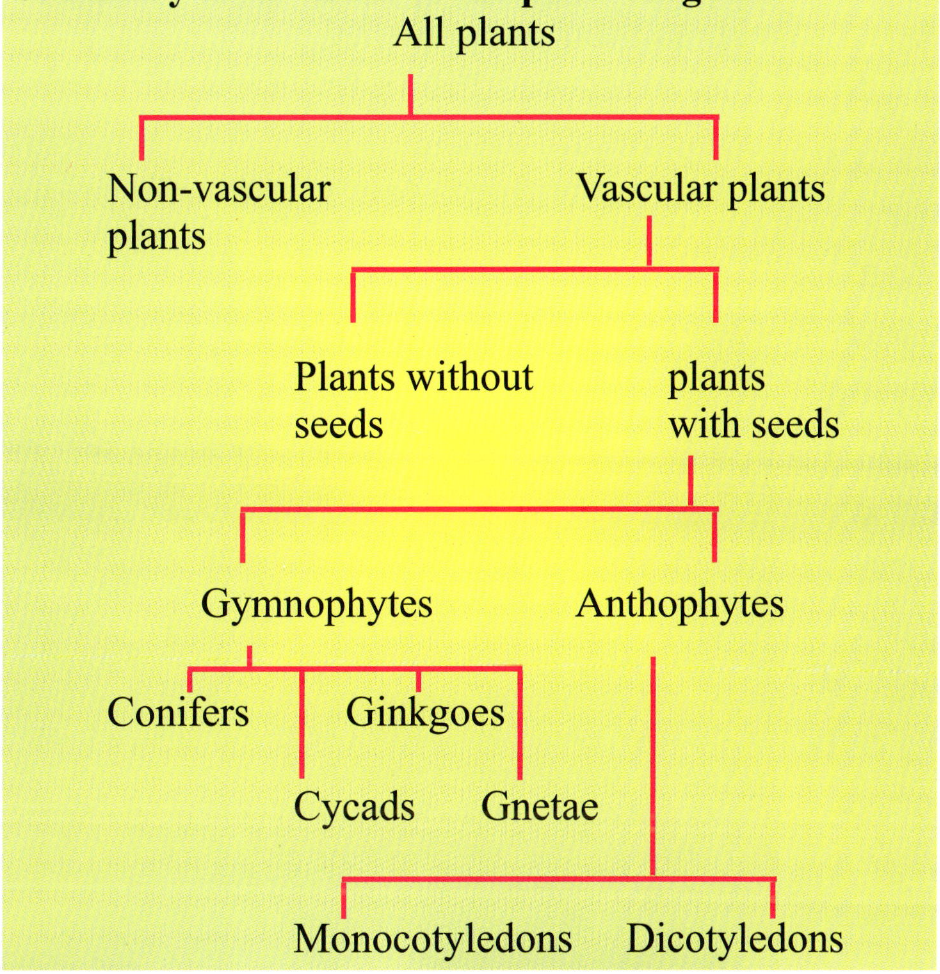

Liverwort

Moss covered trees in rainforest

Terrarium 

A terrarium is a transparent glass or plastic container with soil. It has an open or closed top and is used for displaying growing plants as a miniature landscape. Many kinds of containers can be adapted for terrariums. These clear-sided containers have no drain holes and usually have a clear top.

Plants

Many plants are suitable for growing in terrariums. Low-growing, dense plants are best. Large plants can be used and kept small by pruning. Choose plants for variations in size, texture and color, as well as their adaptability.

Most plants require light near a window or supplemental artificial light. The terrarium should be located within a few metres of a bright window but not in direct sun.

You can plant several types of plants in a terrarium.

Soil

Soil must be high in organic matter, clean and well-drained. Most potting soils sold at nurseries and garden centers have been sterilized. Since terrarium plants are not meant to grow rapidly, adding fertilizer is not necessary.

The soil in a terrarium should be properly moist.

Containers

Almost any type of clear glass or plastic container can be used for a terrarium: fish bowl, fish tank, glass jar, jug or bottle. There are containers made especially for terrariums. The container must be clear, however, as tinted or cloudy glass reduces light and interferes with plant growth. Containers can be closed or open. Plants in closed containers must be tolerant of high humidity. Containers with large openings without covers may be used but will require more frequent watering to maintain humidity.

A properly set terrarium

AMAZING FACT !

The soil in the mix must be sterilized by heating it to a temperature of 95°C.

Planting terrarium

Place a layer of gravel in the bottom of the container for drainage. Next, place a 1-cm layer of horticultural charcoal above the pebbles to keep the soil from developing a sour smell. Sphagnum moss may be placed over the charcoal to prevent soil from sifting into the drainage area.

Add relatively dry soil to the container. To add interest you may choose to arrange the soil so that it slopes from the back of the container towards the front. Remove any leaves that are yellowed, damaged or show any sign of disease or insect damage. Trim the roots of any plants that have a circling rootball. Rocks and wood should be added to the container after the soil. Moist the soil and place the terrarium at the place you want to.

Marsh and Alpine Plants

Marshes are among the most fascinating and diverse wetlands. Often they are named for the most conspicuous vegetation There are cattail, bulrush, sedge, and saw grass marshes, to name just a few. The everglades saw grass marshes in USA are such distinctive subtropical wetlands.

Appearance of marsh plants

Marsh plants are highly varied, yet some look very much alike–especially grasses, sedges, and rushes. Vegetation in a marsh can be divided into three categories: the emergents, the floaters, and the submergents. In many marshes there is a parade of plants, a belting or mosaic of these different growth forms. The progression is sometimes dramatic, with cattails in the shallower water, water lilies floating beyond, and the submerged forms in the deepest water. However, sometimes these vegetation types occur together with shrubs and trees. This condition, in which various wetland types intermingle, is called interspersion. It forms a favorite habitat for waterfowl.

Marsh plantation

Alpine plants

By an alpine plant we mean one whose structure and adaptations allow it to grow in the cold conditions which exist on high mountain sides and summits. Plants which grow on the high summits and wind-swept mountain sides have to face severe climatic conditions. They are, therefore, greatly modified to combat the combined effects of cold, dampness, aridity, strong winds and sunshine.

Alpine plants face severe climatic conditions.

Many alpine plants can be found without the trouble and exertion of climbing. On the more gentle and easier slopes we may find plants as the Trailing Azalea, the Alpine Bear-berry and the Creeping Willow which delight in dry rocky places. The beautiful green springs where bog mosses, and alpine grasses form delightful oases amid the rocks, are the haunts of many lovely little plants; the Alpine Willow-herb, the Alpine Stitchwort and the Starry Saxifrage grow here in profusion.

Alpine plant

AMAZING FACT !

Many mountain plants such as mountain avens, track the sun to warm their flowers, which attracts insects to sunbathe there.

Water Plants

Many plants grow on land, but there are also many aquatic plants. These plants are specially adapted to survive in water. These are called hydrophytes. They vary from microscopic plants, that are found in groups of many millions, to large flowering plants.

Lifestyle of water plants

Water plants are either emergent or submergent. The emergent plants, like reed mace, develop well in very wet soils, or in soil which remains most of the time covered in water. All of their stems and leaves are visible above the surface of the water.

Submergent plants, such as water lilies, grow below the surface of the water. However, some of their parts, such as large leaves, may float on the surface. Unless they are free-floating, their roots, or root-like parts, anchor them to the ground beneath the water.

Water lily has a special feature that enables it to float.

Special characteristics

Water plants have a number of special characteristics, For example, most underwater leaves do not have waxy waterproof coating. This is because the whole leaf surface is required for exchanging gases between the plant and the water. Several aquatic or water plants also have very different leaves above water as well as below the surface.

Many submergent plants develop gaps between the cells in their stems and leaves. These gaps trap air which helps the parts to float.

The gaps between the cells in the leaves help the plant to float in water.

Algae and seaweeds

Algae form a huge group of plants which have a very simple structure . Many kinds of algae are found in water, but they can grow in any suitably damp conditions, as well as in soil, on rocks, and even on living things.

Seaweeds

Seaweeds are multi-celled algae. Most seaweeds have root-like holdfast at their base, which anchor them to solid objects. A few have bubble-like air bladders, which keep them afloat. A seaweed's leaves comprise various pigments which enable them to take in light at different water depths.

Algae

Studying algae

Scientists study the types and numbers of algae in a water sample to find out how clean it is. Single-celled, freshwater algae called desmids are generally found growing in clean water.

Algae in water

AMAZING FACT !

The study of algae is termed phycology, and one who studies algae is known as a phycologist.

Vegetables

Vegetable is a general term for the edible part of a plant. Vegetables are excellent sources of vitamin, iron and calcium. They are sometimes grouped according to the part of the plant they represent. For example, leaves are represented by spinach, seed by peas, etc.

Leafy vegetables

Leafy vegetables represent the leaves of a plant. Some of the vegetables that fall under this category are a spinach, swiss chard, cabbage, etc.

Cabbage

A biennial vegetable from which other brassicas such as cauliflower and broccoli have evolved. The cabbage originated many centuries ago from the European wild cabbage. It has a characteristics tight "head" of leaves. Cabbages can be boiled or pickled or fermented.

Cabbage

Cauliflower

Spinach

Spinach

It is a leafy annual plant widely cultivated as an edible vegetable. Spinach leaves have a relatively high content of iron and vitamin A and C.

Swiss chard

A green leafy vegetable similar to the beet but with an inedible root. Its large leaves, rich in vitamin A, B complex and C, grow throughout the summer.

Swiss chard

Roots and crops

These are the vegetables that grow underground. These vegetables are the roots of a plant. Carrot, beetroot, radish, turnip, all fall under this group of vegetables.

Carrot

It is a biennial vegetables with a swollen, edible root, grown extensively in America and Europe. Its carotene is changed by the body to vitamin A, an essential chemical needed for good vision.

Carrot

Beetroot

Beetroot

Red beets are edible. The white rooted sugar beets provide about 1/3rd of the world's sugar supply. Spinach, beets or chard are used as herbs.

AMAZING FACT !

Broccoli was developed from the wild cabbage in the 17th century in Italy. In the past, gardeners also referred to winter cauliflowers as broccoli and in some areas they may still do so.

Turnip

A plant native to Europe and Asia. It was developed into a root crop, mainly for cattle feed in the 19th century. Its swollen, yellowish white taproot is packed with starch and is fit for human consumption. If left in the ground over the winter, the turnip sends up a flowering stem, using food stored in the root during its first year.

Turnip

More about Vegetables

Vegetable is the edible part of a plant which consists of several minerals and has high nutritional value. Some of the most common vegetables are onion, potato, chillies, brinjal, tomato, etc.

Peas and beans

Peas are herbaceous annual leguminous plant of the pulse family cultivated mainly for its edible seeds. Peas have white or purple flowers and many-seeded fruit pod. It is highly rich in protein. The field pea provides split peas. The sweet pea and chick-pea are of different genera.

Peas

Beans

Pepper

Pepper is better known as capsicum. It is a woody plant of the family Solanaceae, and also is an edible fruit. Commercial garden or bell peppers are grown in warm regions of the World. Red peppers are widely distributed and have been cultivated since pre-Incan times. They include the mild peppers grown and dried for paprika and pungent chilly peppers. Garden peppers are also marketed as unripe green peppers.

Green chilli

Red chilli

Tomatoes

Tomato is a herbaceous plant belonging to the family of nightshade. It is native of South America but was introduced to Europe in the 16th century and is now cultivated worldwide. Most of the crop is canned or processed to make prepared foods. A relatively small proportion of this fruit is being grown for salad use. In northern latitudes, tomatoes are grown under glass but the bulk are grown as a field crop.

Tomato

Pumpkin

Pumpkin

It is the plant of the gourd family. The genus includes winter squashes and summer squashes but the term pumpkin usually refers to the round, orange skinned fruit of the vine. The pumpkin's stringy pulp is used as food and pie filling. The seeds which fill the pumpkin's cavity are also eaten. The pumpkin probably originated in North America.

AMAZING FACT !

Seeds of pepper should be sown in spring in a propagator, set at about 180° C.

Flowers

There are over 250,000 different kinds of flowering plants, including grass, wild flowers, shrubs and trees. Plants which produce flowers are known as anthophytes.

Parts of a flower

Flowers are made-up of many specialized parts. These include petals, stamens (the male parts), and one or more carpels (the female parts). In most plants, the petals are arranged in a circle, around the male and female parts.

Just before a plant blooms, it produces a bud, which eventually develops into a flower. It grows from the expanded tip of a stalk, called the receptacle. Buds are surrounded and protected by small, leaf-like sepals. In some plants, such as buttercups, the sepals remain as a ring around the flower after the bud has opened. In others, such as poppies, they wither and fall off.

Petals are delicate, brightly coloured, and surround the plant's reproductive parts. Some petals are scented or patterned and have areas of cells called nectaries at their base. These produce a sweet, sticky fluid known as nectar, which attracts insects or other animals required for pollination.

Parts of a flower

Male parts

A flower's male reproductive parts are called stamens. Each stamen is made-up of a pod-like anther, at the end of a long stalk called a filament. Anthers contain pollen sacs, which split open to release grains of pollen, the male reproductive cells.

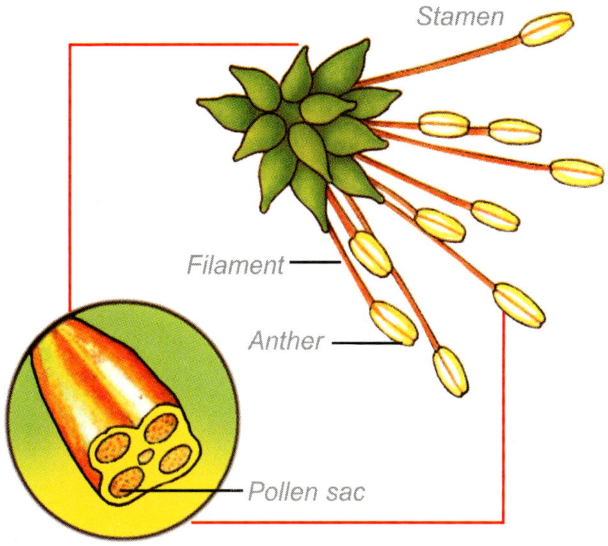

Male parts of a buttercup

Female parts

A flower's female reproductive part is known as the carpel or pistil. It is made-up of the stigma, style and ovary.
The stigma is the top part of a carpel. It has a sticky surface which traps grains of pollen that touch it. The stigma is joined to the ovary by a part of the carpel called the style. Each ovary holds one or more tiny eggs called ovules, which are the female reproductive cells. These develop into seeds after fertilization.

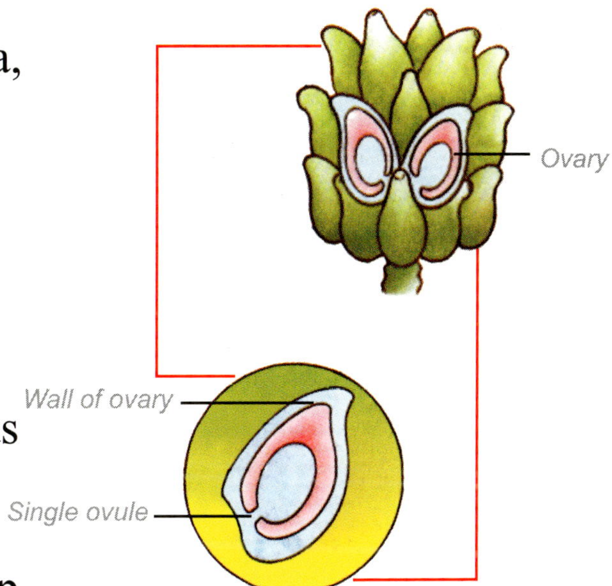

Female parts of a buttercup

Fertilization

In order for a flowering plant to reproduce, the male cell (pollen) and the female cell (ovule) need to join together. This is called fertilization.

AMAZING FACT !

Chinese bell flower's or flowering maple's velvetleaf is cultivated for its fibers called "China Jute". It is used to make rugs.

More about Flowers

Flower is a part of a plant that is concerned with reproduction. Each flower is borne on a stalk or pedicel, the tip of which is expended to form a receptacle that bears floral organs.

Pollination methods

Pollen may be carried from plant to plant by wind, water or animals. When one plant pollinates another plant of the same kind, it is described as cross-pollination. If the pollens grains land on a different type of plant, they don't produce pollen tubes, so pollination can't take place.

Pollination by an insect

Self-pollination

Some types of plants are able to pollinate themselves. This is called self-pollination. For instance, a bee orchid tries to attract a certain type of bee, by looking and smelling like the female species. But if no bees come, the plant's stamens bend over and transfer pollen to its own stigma.

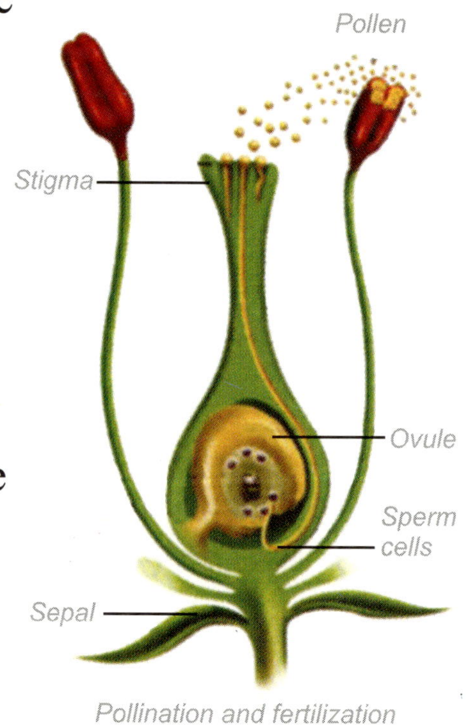

Pollination and fertilization

Animal pollination

Flowers have various ways of attracting animals to carry their pollen. Most have bright coloured petals or sweet scents which attract insects, birds or bats. Many also produce a sweet liquid called nectar, or extra pollen, on which the animals feed. Some have patterns on the petals called nectar guides. These lead the insect into the middle of the flower, where the pollen or nectar can be found. Plants pollinated by animals tend to produce spiky pollen grains. When an animal visits a plant, pollen grains stick to its body. The animal may then transfer these to another flower.

Pollens sticks to this butterfly's body as it feeds from a daisy.

AMAZING FACT !

The daffodil's popularity has resulted in the production of many new varieties in white, pink and orange. Many countries have their national symbols as flowers. The most popular flower is white lily which is the national symbol of nearly 10 countries.

Wind pollination

Wind-pollinated plants rely on the wind to scatter their pollen. They do not need to attract animals, so their flowers are usually unscented, with very small petals and sepals. Some have their male and female parts on separate plants. The male parts hang outside the flowers, allowing their pollen to be carried away more easily.

Fruits

Fertilization in flowering plants leads to the production of seeds. Each seed contains a new developing plant and a store of food. Seeds are kept in part of the plant called a fruit.

Fruits

A fruit is the ripe ovary of a flowering plant containing the seed or seeds. The fruit begins to develop after fertilization. Its main functions are to protect the developing seeds and to help to scatter them when they are ripe. The majority of fruits are formed only from the carpel or carpels of flowers. These fruits are known as true fruits. Some fruits include other parts of the flower, specially the receptacle. These fruits are known as false fruits.

Fruits

Different fruits

Dry fruits and juicy fruits, all come under the category of true fruits. The dry fruits include those that split open and release their seeds and those that do not split open. Juicy fruits also fall into two main groups: the drupes are fruits which are hard and woody, with a single seed inside it. The next are the berries that are juicy fruits that have many seeds in them.

Pomes

Apples and pears belong to a fruit type called'pomes'. These are fruits with a fleshy outer layer and a chambered core that contains a number of seeds. Many of the juicy fruits that we eat are special breeds.

Apple

Pear

Chikoo

AMAZING FACT !

Bananas are odd-shaped berries. Wild bananas have seeds, but the cultivated ones we eat, which are hybrids, seldom have seeds because they are infertile.

Banana

Berries

The tomato and the marrow are berries. Berries are juicy fruits containing many seeds. The cherry is a drupe, also called a stone fruit because the inner layer of the fruit forms a woody 'stone'.The blackberry is a cluster of very small drupes, each containing a tiny stone.

More about Fruits

Fruits with thick, fleshy layers that are often tasty to eat are known as succulent fruit. There are various kinds such as drupes, berries and pomes.

Succulent fruit

Succulent fruits with a single, hard-cased seed in the middle are known as drupes. Plums and cherries are drupes. Succulent fruits that contain several seeds are known as berries. Oranges are berries. Fruit with a thick, fleshy outer cover and a core, with the seeds contained in a capsule, are false fruits known as pomes.

Fruits

Cones

The seeds of conifer trees are contained in cones, not fruit. These develop from the female flowers. After pollination the scales harden and close. When the seeds are ripe and the weather is warm and dry, the scales of the cones open. The seeds flutter out on papery wings. Most of the cones stay on the tree for a year. Others take two years to ripen, and some remain long after the seeds have been dropped.

Cedar cone

Dry fruits

Dry fruits are dry cases that hold the seeds until they are ripe. There are several types. The main ones are described below.

Nuts are dry fruits with only one seed surrounded by a hard shell. Acorns and walnuts are nuts.

Achenes are small-sized, dry fruits comprising a single seed. An achene with papery wings, for example, an ash or sycamore fruit, is called a samara or key fruit. Few achenes, such as ash achenes, grow in bunches. A dry fruit with seeds joined to its inside wall is called as a legume or pod. It splits along its length to open .

A grain, also known as a caryopsis of a kernel, is a small dry fruit whose wall has fused with the seed coat.

Pistachio

Almond

Cashews

Date

Walnut

AMAZING FACT !

Fruit life can be extended by both refrigeration and controlled atmosphere.

Medicinal Plants

It is estimated by the World Health Organization that approximately 75-80 per cent of the world's population uses plant medicines either in part or entirely. For many this is out of necessity, since many cannot afford the high costs of pharmaceutical drugs.

Plants medicines

Historic uses of plant medicines are based upon the traditions of Europeans, Chinese, Egyptians, American Indians, and other cultures and information on plant medicines has been handed down over the centuries. Currently anthropologists and other scientists are investigating newly-discovered cultures (shamans in Amazonia and Belize, for example), to determine what plants are being used. This "ethnobotany" has introduced a number of new compounds into pharmaceutical research.

Medicines

Plants medicines

Activity of plant extracts are first tested in the test tube or in the lab which may indicate major activity in humans. Such test may lead to the discovery of a "wonder drug" herbal medicine responsible for miracle cures. Phytomedicinal prospecting screening plants for biological activity is routinely done today. Huge projects are currently underway by such organizations as INBio, Costa Rica's National Institute of Biodiversity. INBio is cataloging all species of plants and animals in the country - estimated to be around 500,000.

AMAZING FACT !

Guava is used in many ways. It can be made into medicinal teas and jellies.

Lungwort plant

Lungwort

It is a perennial plant that grows in shady areas. Its flowering herb is used medicinally for lung disorders.

Opium

Opium is a narcotic extract derive from the immature fruits of the opium poppy. The milky juice is refined to a powder that has a sharp and bitter taste. A chemical called codeine is derived from this plant that is used for making cough mixtures and many other medicine.

Opium plant

Willow Tree

Willow tree

A common name for about 300 species of tree which occur from the tropics to the arctic. The leaves of this tree helps to give relief in pain.

Quinine

Alkaloid derived from cinchona bark from South America. It was long used in treating a variety of ailments. It was preeminent in early treatment of malaria until the 1930. It is also a mild analgesic and may prevent heart disorder.

Quinine plant

New Plants from Old

Several plants can reproduce by a process in which part of the plant grows into a young one. This process is known as vegetative reproduction or vegetative propagation. This is a type of asexual reproduction which does not involve a male and female sex cell.

Bulbs

Plants like garlic and tulips develop from bulbs. A bulb is a thick, short, underground stem surrounded by scaly leaves that are swollen with food. It stays alive over winter when the remaining plant dies. A bulb can reproduce asexually by sprouting new bulbs on the side.

Onion

Garlic

Runners

Some plants, like the spider plant and strawberry plant, can reproduce by forming long side shoots called runners or stolons. When the runners reach the ground, they produce roots of their own, and begin to develop into young ones. At first the new plant is fed by the parent, but once it can live on its own, the runner rots away.

Growing up

Vegetative reproduction develops much rapidly than they can develop from seed. The new ones are identical to the parent plant. Farmers and gardeners often make use of a plant's ability to reproduce vegetatively. As well as producing more plants, they know that the new plants will be of the same quality as the parent plant.

Growers have also discovered new ways of removing parts from a plant to grow young ones. These are a few examples of artificial propagation as, left to themselves, plants usually do not reproduce by these methods.

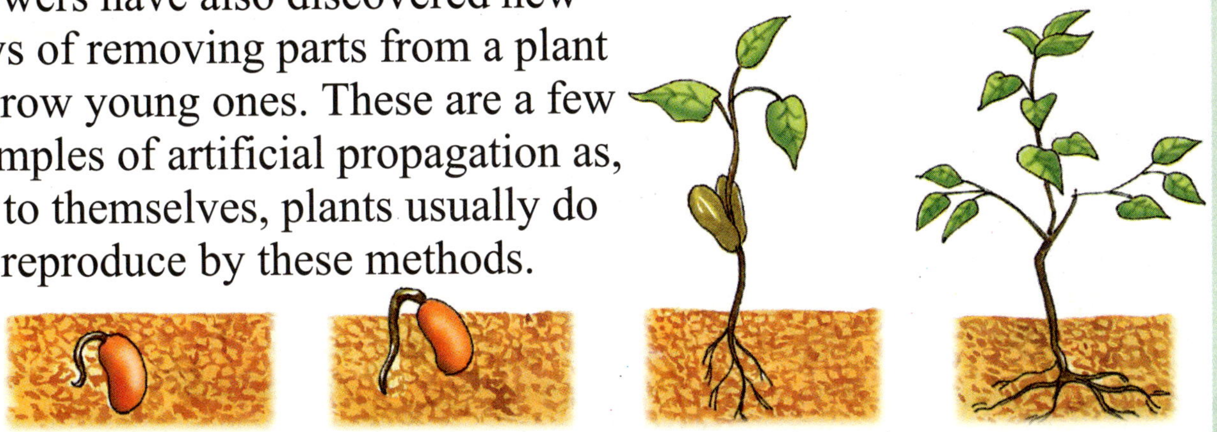

A single seed can develop into a big plant within a few weeks.

Taking cuttings

One common procedure of artificial propagation is cutting. This includes taking a piece like a side stem or leaf off a plant and planting it in soil where it develops into a young one. The cutting may require to stay in water for some time to grow before being planted in soil.

A piece of plant is cut from a parent plant.

The cutting is placed in water until roots begin to grow.

The cutting is re-planted in soil.

AMAZING FACT!

Garlic bulbs are composite bulbs. This means that each swollen leaf, called a clove can grow into a garlic plant.

Plants and People

Our Earth can be divided into biomes. Each is a area with a matchless climate and type of soil. A biome supports ecosystems groups of plants and animals which interact with each other and their surroundings. Several ecosystems are harmed by the way people use the land.

Food for all

Cattle gazing in a field

For thousands of years, humans used several methods of producing the food they needed from the land they lived on.

But as the population grew, more and more food was required. This meant using more space to grow crops, or using existing farmland more efficiently. Some farming procedures had a disastrous effect on ecosystems, though.
Since farming started, people have identified plants with useful features, like bigger fruit or better resistance to pests, and have used their seeds to grow better crops, This is known as selective breeding. Overuse of selective breeding may lead to a loss of biodiversity - the huge variety of living things on Earth.

Field Farming

Organic farming

Organic farming works closely with nature by not adding artificial chemicals to the soil, For instance, instead of using chemical pesticides, some organic farmers plant onions among their crops. The strong smell of onions masks the smell of the crops; the pests are not attracted.

Organic farmers often use a method called crop rotation. Crops which use or replace certain minerals, such as nitrates, are planted in different fields each year. Manure and compost are used as fertilizers to help the crops to grow. This method keeps levels of natural substances balanced in the soil.

AMAZING FACT!

By clearing large areas for farmland, there is a danger that we are losing too many natural habitats, including hedgerows and woodland.

Organic farming

FASCINATING FACTS

- In 1665, 7,000 people died every week in London because of bubonic plague, also called the black death.
- A long time ago, people believed a skeleton or a skeletal bird symbolized the coming of the plague, but it is not true.
- If a bacteria divides every 15 minutes there will be 4.096 × 10 to the 28th power bacteria at the end of 24 hours.
- Your body is composed of one hundred trillion cells. For every, one human cell, your body has 100 bacterial cells.
- To transport cowpox as a vaccine against smallpox, early colonists would put one hundred and fifty children on a boat and ship them across the ocean. One child would be deliberately infected with the cowpox virus. That child would spread it to the others. By the time they got to their destination, a vaccine could be acquired from children who had just recently caught the disease.
- Diatoms (microscopic one-celled organisms) created the Earth's atmosphere (or at least most of the oxygen in it).
- A virus cannot reproduce by itself.

- People used to believe that when you sneezed, your spirit would leave your body for a little while and allow bad spirits to enter, and that's why you say "Bless You" when somebody sneezes.

- In 1097, Trotula, a midwife of Salerno, wrote *The Diseases of Women*- it was used in medical schools for 600 years.

- If a statue of a person on a horse has both front legs in the air, the person died in battle; if the horse has one front leg in the air, the person died as a result of wounds received in battle; if the horse has all four legs on the ground, like the Zizkov Monument, the person died of natural causes.

- When Leonardo da Vinci's Mona Lisa was stolen from the Louvre in1912, 6 replicas were sold as the original, each at a huge price, in the 3 years before the original was recovered.

- 2 billion people still cannot read.

- The problem of missing teeth was first discussed at length in 1728 by Pierre Fauchard in his book *The Surgeon Dentist*.

- Although the Aardvark is endemic to Africa and shares some similarities with the South American anteater, the two are not related. Hearing and sense of smell is acute but eyesight is poor. Tongue is sticky and can reach 45cm from the mouth. Eats primarily termites and ants.

- The African Golden Cat is a medium sized cat and can grow to 90cm in body length and weigh up to 18kg. Apart from duika and other small antelope it is thought that the main part of the golden cats diet is made-up of rodents, tree hyraxes and birds.

- The Andean Mountain Cat is to be found in the high regions of Bolivia, Peru and Chile. The mountain cat is slightly larger than a big domestic cat, growing up to 60cm in length with a tail of some 70 per cent of its body length.

- Ants carry 10 times their body weight. Worker ants live one to five years; some queens live longer that 20 years. The biggest ant colony found was on the Ishikari Coast of Hokkaido: 306 million ants, with 1,080,000 queens in 45,000 interconnected nests over an area of 2.7 sq. km.

- The bee is a remarkable animal-they do not have ears, but they have an excellent sense of smell with chemoreceptors in their antennae. Bees see colours differently than we do. They are insensitive to red but detects ultraviolet light which is invisible to us.

- The Library of Congress, the largest library in the world, stores 18 million books on approximately 850 km of bookshelves. The collections include 119 million items, 2 million recordings, 12 million photographs, 4 million maps and 53 million manuscripts.